U0738626

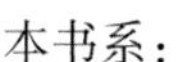

本书系：

江西理工大学华文教育研究中心招标课题（WYHW201501）阶段性成果

“魅力汉语·悦读经典”丛书

英汉对照

中国经典神话故事

Chinese Classic Myths

李火秀 邓 琳◎编著

总　序

伴随着我国经济的快速发展和国际联系的日益密切，世界范围内“汉语热”的持续升温，汉语教育也呈现出强劲的发展势头。世界各地的华文教育，正以前所未有的速度向前推进。当前，华文教育的内容、范畴、功能、目标都从单一走向多元，华文教育教学不仅注重汉语的语音、词汇、语法、汉字等中文基础知识的讲解，而且还以弘扬中华文化、形塑中国形象、提升华人的民族文化素质与文化认同，促进中外文化交流，增进中外友谊为重要目标。中华文化及相关内涵精神的独特魅力，通过华文教育教学，获得了海外华人以及越来越多非华裔外国人的了解、熟悉及应用，中华文化及其所蕴含的普适性价值在异域大放光彩。基于此，海外同胞把华文教育当作“留根工程”，同时也是提高后代素质，参与竞争的“希望工程”，其意义重大而深远。

在这一新形势下，我校（江西理工大学）始终坚持开放办学的思想，在教育国际化和华文教育工作方面取得了可喜成绩。截至目前，我校与美国、英国、法国、韩国、日本、泰国等 20 多个国家的高校和企业建立了交流与合作关系。其中，与泰国宋卡王子大学的合作交流，早在二十年前就已经展开，双方每年都开展多次师生互访并联合培养博士、硕士研究生。近年来，面对国内外华文教育迅猛的发展形势，我校于 2008 年创办对外汉语专业(后更名为汉语国际教育)；2011 年 11 月，国务院侨务办公室下发《关于同意江西理工大学建立华文教育基地的批复》的文件，使我校成为江西第二个、赣州第一个华文教育基地；2012 年 3 月，我校外语外贸学院成立了“江西理工大学华文教育研究中心”；2014 年 12 月，学校同意将研究中心升级为校级科研平台进行管理和建设；2015 年我校与巴基斯坦旁遮普大学签署共建孔子学院的协议，实现了我校在海外设立孔子学院的重大历史性突破。所有这些喜人的成绩离不开我校各级领导在华文教育

教学和管理工作方面的夙夜在公、殚精竭虑；离不开所有教师的恪尽职守、勤勉敬业；离不开所有与华文教育教学工作相关教师的勠力同心、砥砺奋进。当然，我们深知中华传统文化博大精深，要将我国传统文化发扬光大，使传统文化在当代引起共鸣与认同，我们责无旁贷，任重而道远。

为此，我们编写了一套“魅力汉语·悦读经典”丛书，精选中华传统文化、文学中最经典、最有价值的神话传说、寓言故事等。本套丛书为了便于读者能够独立阅读，在保持原著精髓的基础上，采用平实流畅、简洁生动的语言讲述故事。每篇故事均配汉语拼音、中英文对照、故事寓意的品读，并且每篇都绘制了一幅精美插图。另外，丛书对一些生难字词做了中英文注释。这些都可以让读者增强阅读印象，更好地领略经典名作的魅力，体验人类最高尚的情感和最珍贵的品质，进而提升知识理解水平和审美鉴赏能力，获得心灵的滋养和精神的洗礼。

本套丛书不仅可以成为汉语学习者学习汉语、理解中华文化的专门读本，也可以成为英语学习者扩大阅读视野、提升英语水平的专门文本。当然，丛书中精选的内容同样可以成为广大文学爱好者品读经典，了解中国传统文化的通识读物。

General Preface

With the rapid development of the booming economy and the increasingly closer international connections, the popularity of learning Mandarin is spreading worldwide, which shows a strong development tendency. Chinese language and culture education in the world is developing rapidly at an unprecedented speed. Currently, the content, category, function and goal of Chinese language and culture education have developed from unitary to multiple. It does not only focus on imparting Chinese phonetics, vocabulary, grammar, and Chinese characters, but also aims to advance the Chinese culture, shape China's image in the world, improve the overseas Chinese people's national cultural literacy and identity, promote the sino-foreign cultural exchange and strengthen the sino-foreign friendship. Chinese culture and the charm of its connotations are understood, well known and used by more and more overseas Chinese and some non-Chinese foreigners through the Chinese language and culture education. The universal values of Chinese culture are shining brightly overseas. Besides, overseas Chinese regard

the Chinese language and culture education as the "Root Project" and the "Hope Project" which aims at improving the descendants' cultural literacy, carrying great and profound significance.

In this new situation, Jiangxi University of Science and Technology insists on the running of open education and had made great achievements on international education as well as the Chinese language and culture education. Till now, our school has set up collaboration relationships with universities and enterprises in more than 20 countries like the US, the UK, France, Korea (R. O.), Japan, Thailand, etc. The collaboration with Prince of Songkla University started twenty years ago. Each year, there are many times of exchanging visits for teachers and students in our school and Prince of Songkla University which co-cultivate doctoral candidates and postgraduates with our school. In recent years, to meet the rapid development of Chinese language and culture education, in 2008, our school began to recruit students majoring in Teaching Chinese as a Foreign Language which was renamed as Chinese International Education later. On November, 2011, the Overseas Chinese Affairs Office issued the

file "Approval of Jiangxi University of Science and Technology as the Chinese Language and Culture Education Base" which enabled our school to be the second one in Jiangxi Province and the first in the city of Ganzhou as the education base. On March, 2012, our faculty set up "The Research Center of Chinese Language and Culture Education" which was upgraded to the research platform of our school on December, 2014. Later, in 2015, our school set up the Confucius Institute with Pakistan's Punjab University, making a historic breakthrough. All these achievements are attributed to the hard work of leaders at all levels in our school and particularly those teachers working for the Chinese language and culture education. Of course, we surely know the extensiveness and profoundness of traditional Chinese culture. So we will spare no effort and take the responsibility to promote and develop Chinese traditional culture, gaining more acceptance and resonance for it in the contemporary world. We have the duty to spread it and develop it.

For this purpose, we compiled this series of books named "Charming Chinese, Classic Reading", in which the most classic, valuable stories

about Chinese traditional culture, literature, myths and fables were selected. To enable readers to do the reading alone, all the stories are edited with plain, concise but vivid words. Every story in both Chinese and English goes with Chinese characters and the corresponding pinyin. A vivid picture is drawn at the beginning of each story which ends with the story's comment. Besides, notes are given for some difficult words. In this way, readers may have a joyful reading experience in which they can appreciate the charm of the classics, the noblest emotions and the precious characters of humans, which in turn will help them improve their comprehensive and aesthetic appreciation ability and eventually receive spiritual nourishment and baptism.

This series of books render learners of Chinese a way to learn Chinese language and culture, broaden their reading vision and improve their English reading ability. Meanwhile, these books can be a good choice for those lovers of literature to learn Chinese traditional culture.

前　言

神话是原始先民在长期的社会实践中孕育并创造出来的一种文学艺术，它以感性、丰盈、优美与诗意的想象，再现了人类最初的社会生活和精神面貌。 中华民族的神话故事源远流长，它们是中华文明产生和发展的源头，更是全人类文明的重要组成部分、世界文学艺术宝库中的奇葩。

中华民族的神话故事丰富多彩。 从具体内容上来看，大致可划分为创世神话、人类起源、发明创造、神佛、英雄神话等。 在此，我们将这种划分略做说明：

（1）创世神话。 它是原始先民对宇宙天地来源的天才式想象，它追问世界的起源。 在中国神话故事里，盘古因为他开天辟地的英雄伟业，成了中华民族最重要的神之一。

（2）人类起源。 它探索在天地开辟以后，人类是怎么诞生的。 在中国神话体系中，女娲是抟土造人的神，而且她牺牲自我，提炼五彩石补天的感人事迹，使原始先民将她看作是亲切仁爱的守护神。

(3) 发明创造。原始先民对社会生活中各式各样的日常用物、医药、汉字、节日庆典、神的诞生等给予丰富的想象，如燧人氏钻木取火、伏羲琴的创造、神农尝百草、仓颉造字、嫘祖养蚕、杜康酿酒、门神由来、茶神陆羽、十二生肖的故事等，皆是人类对所用物、自然现象、神造物等的想象。

(4) 神佛、英雄神话。记录了天神、英雄等的伟大事迹，如夸父逐日、后羿射日、大禹治水、精卫填海、刑天舞干戚等。这些神明、英雄皆是神力过人、武艺超群、勇敢侠义的人物，受到人们的崇敬。这些英雄人物身上，寄托了人类渴望征服自然的愿望。

总之，中国神话作为人类童年时代的产物之一，其构建出的纯真艺术形象和朴素的风格，展露出人类对完美自我的殷切期待、对理想生存方式与生命形式的深情召唤。它们所散发的蓬勃艺术生命力能够穿越时空隧道，不断吸引着人们去阅读，去欣赏。

本书精选了中国神话故事中最具有代表性、最经典的作品，包括了宇宙天地的开辟、人类的起源、神的诞生、神的家族、神造物的传说，以及流传深广的英雄神话、人神相恋等优美故事。本书采用故事加注拼音与中英文对照、生难字词中英文注释的方式，以精练语言讲述故事，加入精彩的故事品读，并根据情节配以精美的插图。力图将一个诗意盎然、浪漫动人的神话世界全方位、多层次地展现在读者面前，让读者在阅读故事时获得酣畅淋漓的审美体验和审美愉悦。

品读神话经典，构织精彩人生，让生命在阅读中得到升华，让人生在阅读中更加充实。

编　者

2016 年 1 月 5 日

Preface

Myth is a literary art form created by primitive people through long time of social practice. With its sensibility, abundance, beautiful and poetic image, it shows the social and spiritual life of ancient men. Chinese nation's myths, with a long history, breed Chinese civilization. They are precious treasures of the world literature and art, as well as an important part of human civilization.

The rich and colorful Chinese myths can be roughly divided into several categories, such as legends of genesis, origin of humans, invention and creation, gods and Buddhas, heroic stories, etc. As to these categories, the following explanations are needed:

(1) Legends of genesis: the answers given by primitive people to their puzzle towards the origin of the universe and the world. In Chinese myths, Pangu is worshiped as an important god for his creation of the world.

(2) Origin of humans: the exploration of how human beings appeared in the world. In Chinese myths, Nüwa is the goddess who creates human beings with soil. She is the patron saint of the Chinese people for her selfless labor of

(3) Invention and creation: primitive people had a rich imagination towards daily stuff like medicines, Chinese characters, festivals and celebrations, the birth of gods, etc., which resulted in myths such as Suiren Drilling Wood to Make a Fire, Fuxi Cutting Phoenix Tree and Making Peptachord, Shennong Discovering the Curative Virtues of Plants, Cangjie Inventing Chinese Characters, Silkworm Goddess Leizu, Dukang Making Wine, The Origin of Door Gods, Tea God Lu Yu and The 12 Animals of the Chinese Zodiac. All the stories show people's rich imagination towards the things they used, natural phenomenon, and things created by gods.

(4) Gods, Buddhas, and heroic stories: The heroic acts of gods and heroes are recorded, like Kuafu Racing with the Sun, Houyi Shooting the Renegade Suns, Yu Harnessing the Flood, The Bird Jingwei Filling the Sea, Xingtian Brandishing Ganqi. These gods and heroes are all full of superpower, strength, braveness and righteousness. They are respected and admired by people. From them, you can see the wishes of primitive people who were eager to conquer the nature.

In short, Chinese myths are one of the products of humans' childhood. The pure art image and simple art style show humans' hoping for the perfect and pure, and their longing for an ideal way of living. The charm of Chinese myths will linger in time and space, attracting more and more people to read and enjoy them.

The stories selected are the most classic and typical works, covering the creating of the world, the origin of humans, the birth of gods, the family of gods, the gods' creating of substances, the heroic myths, the love between the goddesses and common people. Each story in both Chinese and English goes with pinyin and notes for difficult words. With refined words, story comments and vivid illustrations, each myth shows readers a poetic, romantic and touching myth world with rich diversity, rendering readers joyful experience and aesthetic pleasure.

Reading classic myths will enrich your colorful life with great fulfillment.

Compilers

January 5th, 2016

目　录
Contents

第一辑
Part 1

盘古开天辟地

Pangu Creating the World / 3

女娲抟土造人

Nüwa Creating Human Beings with Soil / 8

女娲补天

Nüwa Patching Up the Sky / 14

燧人氏钻木取火

Suiren Drilling Wood to Make a Fire / 20

年的来历

The Origin of "Nian" / 26

十二生肖的传说

The 12 Animals of the Chinese Zodiac / 32

神农尝百草

Shennong Discovering the Curative Virtues of Plants / 36

仓颉造字

Cangjie Inventing Chinese Characters / 41

伏羲伐桐制瑶琴

Fuxi Cutting Phoenix Tree to Make Peptachord / 47

门神由来

The Origin of Door Gods / 53

蚕神嫘祖

Silkworm Goddess Leizu / 59

茶神陆羽

Tea God Lu Yu / 63

第二辑
Part 2

大禹治水

Yu Harnessing the Flood / 71

精卫填海

The Bird Jingwei Filling the Sea / 76

愚公移山

Yugong Removing the Mountains / 81

后羿射日

Houyi Shooting the Renegade Suns / 86

杜康酿酒

Dukang Making Wine / 91

杜鹃啼血

The Cuckoo Crying Blood / 96

观音送画

Goddess Guanyin Sending Pictures / 100

尧舜禅让

Yao and Shun Abdicating and Handing Over the Crown / 106

夸父逐日

Kuafu Racing with the Sun / 110

刑天舞干戚

Xingtian Brandishing Ganqi / 114

鲤鱼跳龙门

Carp Jumping over the Dragon Gate / 119

二月二龙抬头

February 2, the "Dragon Rise" / 124

第三辑
Part 3

月下老人
The Old Man under the Moon / 131
天仙配
The Marriage of the Fairy Princess / 136
牛郎织女
The Cowherd and the Girl Weaver / 140
孟姜女哭长城
Seeking Her Husband at the Great Wall / 146
嫦娥奔月
The Goddess Chang'e's Ascending to the Moon / 152
沉香救母
Chenxiang Rescuing His Mother / 157
哪吒闹海
Prince Nezha's Triumph Against Dragon King / 162
八仙过海
The Eight Immortals Crossing the Sea / 167
神女峰
Goddess Peak / 171
神笔马良
Ma Liang and His Magic Brush / 177
田螺姑娘
The River Snail Maiden / 182
百鸟朝凤
Hundred Birds Paying Homage to the Phoenix / 187

后 记
Postscript / 192

中国经典神话故事

第一辑

Part 1

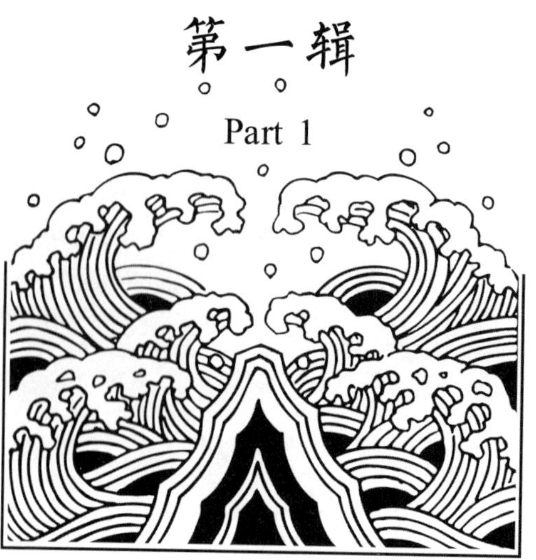

盘古开天辟地

Pangu Creating the World

yuǎn gǔ shí qī yǔ zhòu tiān dì yí piàn hùn dùn jiù xiàng yí gè dà
远古时期，宇宙天地一片混沌，就像一个大

jī dàn yí yàng jù rén pán gǔ zài zhè ge dà jī dàn zhōng shuì zháo le
鸡蛋一样。巨人盘古在这个大鸡蛋中睡着了。

dà gài guò le yí wàn bā qiān duō nián dāng tā shuì xǐng le zhēng kāi yǎn jing
大概过了一万八千多年，当他睡醒了，睁开眼睛

de shí hou què fā xiàn zhōu wéi hēi hū hū de shén me yě kàn bú jiàn yú
的时候，却发现周围黑乎乎的，什么也看不见。于

shì tā bá xià zì jǐ de yì kē yá chǐ bǎ tā biàn chéng yì bǎ jù dà de
是，他拔下自己的一颗牙齿，把它变成一把巨大的

fǔ tóu yòng lì xiàng zhōu wéi pī kǎn zhōng yú bǎ zhè piàn hùn dùn fēn kāi lái
斧头，用力向周围劈砍，终于把这片混沌分开来

le qīng de qì wǎng shàng fēi xíng chéng tiān zhòng de wǎng xià chén xíng chéng
了，轻的气往上飞形成天，重的往下沉形成
le dì
了地。

rán ér tiān yǔ dì fēn kāi hòu suí jí yòu màn màn hé lǒng pán gǔ jiù
然而，天与地分开后随即又慢慢合拢，盘古就
yòng shǒu zhǎng chēng zhù tiān kōng shuāng jiǎo yòng lì cǎi zhe dà dì nǔ lì
用手掌撑住天空，双脚用力踩着大地，努力
de bú ràng tiān kōng yā dào dì miàn shang rì fù yí rì nián fù yì nián
地不让天空压到地面上。日复一日，年复一年，
shí jiān guò qù le yí wàn bā qiān nián zhōng yú pán gǔ kě yǐ jiāng shēn tǐ
时间过去了一万八千年。终于，盘古可以将身体
tǐng zhí gāo jǔ shuāng shǒu bǎ tiān kōng xiàng shàng tuō le tā de shēn tǐ měi guò
挺直，高举双手把天空向上托了，他的身体每过
yì tiān zhǎng gāo yí zhàng tiān yǔ dì yě yì tiān lí kāi yí zhàng tiān shēng de
一天长高一丈，天与地也一天离开一丈，天升得
yuè gāo pán gǔ de shēn qū yě biàn de yuè cháng tiān dì bèi tā chēng kāi le
越高，盘古的身躯也变得越长。天地被他撑开了
jiǔ wàn lǐ tā yě zhǎng chéng le yí gè gāo jiǔ wàn lǐ de jù rén
九万里，他也长成了一个高九万里的巨人。

zuì hòu tiān yǔ dì de wèi zhì bèi láo láo gù dìng le kě shì pán gǔ
最后，天与地的位置被牢牢固定了。可是盘古
yě lèi kuǎ le tā kàn zhe chuàng zào chū de tiān dì shì jiè wēi xiào zhe dǎo
也累垮了。他看着创造出的天地世界，微笑着倒
xià qù zài yě méi yǒu qǐ lái zài tā dǎo xià qù de yí chà nà tā de
下去，再也没有起来。在他倒下去的一刹那，他的
zuǒ yǎn biàn chéng le tài yáng yòu yǎn biàn chéng le yuè liang tóu fa hé hú
左眼变成了太阳，右眼变成了月亮，头发和胡
xū biàn chéng le xīng xing gǔ gé biàn chéng le shān mài hé qiū líng ròu shēn
须变成了星星，骨骼变成了山脉和丘陵，肉身

biàn chéng le píng yuán hé pén dì xuè hé hàn shuǐ biàn chéng le jiāng hǎi hú
变成了平原和盆地，血和汗水变成了江海湖

pō máo fà biàn chéng le bù mǎn dà dì de huā cǎo shù mù tā hū chū de
泊，毛发变成了布满大地的花草树木。他呼出的

qì tǐ biàn chéng le fēng hé yún wù fā chū de shēng yīn biàn chéng le léi
气体变成了风和云雾，发出的声音变成了雷

míng cóng nà yǐ hòu rén shì jiān yǒu le yáng guāng yǔ lù dà dì shang
鸣。从那以后，人世间有了阳光雨露，大地上

shēng jī àng rán
生机盎然。

In ancient times, the sky and the earth were at first chaos, like an egg in which Pangu had slept for about 18,000 years before he woke up and saw the black, dark emptiness of the universe. Then, he pulled out a tooth from his mouth and turned it into an enormous sharp axe, chopping around with the greatest strength. Finally, the blurred entity was separated. The light rose to become the sky while the heavy sank to form the earth.

However, after the separation, the sky and the earth slowly closed again. Pangu stood between the sky and the earth with his hands holding up the sky and his feet stepping on the earth. Day after day, year after year, it was after eighteen thousand years when Pangu could finally square his shoulders and held up the sky highly with his hands. Each day, the sky and the earth were separated by 1 *zhang* (ten units of length) with 1 *zhang*'s growth of his body. His body grew longer as the sky rose higher. Eventually, the sky and the earth were separated for ninety thousand *li* while Pangu grew into a ninety thousand *li* -tall giant.

But Pangu was so tired that he fell down with a smile for seeing the created new world and never stood up again. No sooner had he fallen down than his left eye became the sun and the right eye turned into the moon; his hair and beard became the stars; his bones became the mountains and hills; his flesh became the plains and basins; his blood and sweat became the rivers and lakes; his body hair became the trees and plants on the earth; his breath became the winds and clouds; his voice became the thunder. From then on, the earth was full of sunshine, rain and life.

生难字/词注解 | Notes

盘古：人名。

Pangu (name): Creator of the universe in Chinese myths.

混沌：盘古开天辟地之前天地模糊一团的状态。

Chaos: The primeval state of the universe, before Pangu separated the sky and the earth.

劈砍：用刀斧等猛剁，用力劈开。

Chop: Use an enormous sharp axe to separate the object fiercely with strength.

故事点评 | Story Comment

盘古具有超人的神奇力量和无私奉献的伟大精神，他为人类开辟天地，带来光明，成为中华民族崇拜的英雄。

Pangu had magic superhuman power and strength as well as the great selfless spirit of devotion. He created the world and brought light for humans. He became a hero worshiped by the Chinese nation.

女娲抟土造人

Nüwa Creating Human Beings with Soil

pán gǔ bǎ tiān yǔ dì kāi pì yǐ hòu rén shì jiān yǒu le rì yuè xīng
盘古把天与地开辟以后，人世间有了日月星
chén huā cǎo shù mù hé niǎo shòu chóng yú kě shì què méi yǒu rén lèi yǒu
辰、花草树木和鸟兽虫鱼，可是却没有人类。有
yí gè shén tōng guǎng dà de nǚ shén jiào zuò nǚ wā chuán shuō tā yì tiān
一个神通广大的女神，叫作女娲，传说她一天
dāng zhōng néng gòu biàn huà qī shí cì tā fā xiàn rén jiān jì liáo de jǐng
当中能够变化七十次。她发现人间寂寥的景
xiàng gǎn dào fēi cháng gū dú tā jué de zài zhè tiān dì zhī jiān yīng gāi
象，感到非常孤独。她觉得在这天地之间，应该
yòng shén me dōng xi jiāng tā tián sāi qǐ lái zhè yàng cái néng gòu bó fā shēng
用什么东西将它填塞起来，这样才能够勃发生

jī yú shì tā kāi shǐ sì chù xún zhǎo tā zǒu a zǒu a shí zài shì
机。于是，她开始四处寻找，她走啊走啊，实在是

tài lèi le jiù zài yí gè hú pō páng biān tíng xià lái qīng chè de hú shuǐ zhào
太累了，就在一个湖泊旁边停下来，清澈的湖水照

jiàn le tā de miàn róng hé shēn yǐng tā xiào shuǐ lǐ de yǐng zi yě xiàng zhe
见了她的面容和身影。她笑，水里的影子也向着

tā xiào tā jiǎ zhuāng shēng qì shuǐ lǐ de yǐng zi yě xiàng zhe tā shēng qì
她笑；她假装生气，水里的影子也向着她生气。

tā hū rán xiǎng dào suī rán shì jiān gè zhǒng gè yàng de shēng wù dōu yǒu
她忽然想到：“虽然，世间各种各样的生物都有

le kě dān dān méi yǒu xiàng zì jǐ yí yàng de shēng wù nà wèi shén me bú
了，可单单没有像自己一样的生物，那为什么不

chuàng zào yì zhǒng xiàng zì jǐ yí yàng de shēng wù ne
创造一种像自己一样的生物呢？”

yú shì nǚ wā jué xīn yào zào rén tā cóng chí táng páng biān jué qǐ
于是，女娲决心要造人。她从池塘旁边掘起

yì tuán huáng ní jiā shuǐ jiǎo yún jiāng tā róu niē chéng yí gè xiǎo ní rén
一团黄泥，加水搅匀，将它揉捏成一个小泥人。

nǚ wā cháo zhe nà ge xiǎo ní rén chuī kǒu qì nà ge xiǎo ní rén biàn huó
女娲朝着那个小泥人吹口气，那个小泥人便“活”

le qǐ lái biàn chéng le yí gè néng zhàn néng zǒu ér qiě huì shuō huà de
了起来，变成了一个能站、能走，而且会说话的

xiǎo wá wa xiǎo wá wa zhàn zài dì shang bèng bèng tiào tiào kāi xīn de jiào
小娃娃。小娃娃站在地上蹦蹦跳跳，开心地叫

nǚ wā wéi mā ma nǚ wā kàn zhe zhè ge cōng míng kě ài de xiǎo wá
女娲为“妈妈”。女娲看着这个聪明可爱的小娃

wa fēi cháng gāo xìng gěi tā qǔ le yí gè míng zi rén
娃，非常高兴，给她取了一个名字：“人”。

nǚ wā duì yú tā de zuò pǐn gǎn dào hěn mǎn yì dàn shì nǚ wā
女娲对于她的作品，感到很满意。但是，女娲

jué de yí gè shēng wù tài gū dān le yú shì tā xiǎng ràng gèng duō de
觉得一个生物太孤单了。于是，她想让更多的
shēng wù bù mǎn dà dì jiù bù fēn zhòu yè de yòng huáng ní róu niē xǔ duō
生物布满大地，就不分昼夜地用黄泥揉捏许多
kě ài de xiǎo rénr zhè xiē xiǎo rénr yì jiē chù dì miàn jiù huó le
可爱的小人儿。这些小人儿一接触地面就活了，
dà shēng de hū hǎn mā ma cóng cǐ tā zài yě bù gǎn dào gū dú
大声地呼喊“妈妈”。从此，她再也不感到孤独、
jì mò le tā bù tíng de niē zhe niē zhe bù zhī bù jué yǐ dào le yè
寂寞了。她不停地捏着捏着，不知不觉已到了夜
wǎn tā shí zài shì tài lèi le bǎ tóu zhěn zài shān yá shang shuì zháo le
晚，她实在是太累了，把头枕在山崖上睡着了。

dì èr tiān tiān gāng gāng liàng tā gǎn jǐn qǐ lái jì xù gōng zuò
第二天，天刚刚亮，她赶紧起来继续工作。
tā yì xīn yào ràng zhè xiē líng mǐn de xiǎo shēng wù bù mǎn dà dì rán ér
她一心要让这些灵敏的小生物布满大地。然而，
tiān dì tài dà bù jiǔ tā yǐ jīng hěn kǔ hěn lèi le hòu lái tā xiǎng chū
天地太大，不久她已经很苦很累了。后来她想出
yí gè bàn fǎ cóng shān yá shang lā chě yì tiáo téng màn shēn rù ní tán
一个办法，从山崖上拉扯一条藤蔓，伸入泥潭
zhān shàng ní jiāng xiàng dì miàn huī sǎ ní diǎn jiàn luò de dì fang jiù
沾上泥浆，向地面挥洒，泥点溅落的地方，就
chū xiàn xǔ duō huó líng huó xiàn de xiǎo rénr yí huìr shí jiān dà dì
出现许多活灵活现的小人儿。一会儿时间，大地
shang jiù bù mǎn le rén lèi de zōng jì nǚ wā bǎ nà xiē rén fēn wéi nán
上就布满了人类的踪迹。女娲把那些人分为男
hé nǚ ràng tā men zì yóu jié hé fán yǎn hòu dài cóng cǐ rén lèi jiù
和女，让他们自由结合，繁衍后代。从此，人类就
zhè yàng shì shì dài dài chuán chéng bù xī
这样世世代代传承不息。

After the creation of the world by Pangu, there appeared the sun and the moon, plants, birds, beasts, worms and fish but no human on earth. A goddess with magical power named Nüwa could change her form for seventy times a day. She felt lonely seeing the silent scene on earth, believing between the sky and the earth there should be something making the earth lively. Then she walked around and searched for the thing that could bring liveliness to the earth. She walked without stop until she felt so tired that she stopped by a lake where her image was reflected. She smiled to the image in the water while the latter smiled back to her. She pretended to be angry to the image while the latter became angry with her. It inspired her that there were all kinds of creatures on earth except the ones like her. Why not make some creatures like her?

Then she decided to create mankind. By a pool, she dug some soil, mixed it with water, and kneaded a little clay figurine by hand. Nüwa puffed to the little clay figurine which incredibly came alive, stood up, walked around and even talked. It jumped and danced happily on the ground, yelling the goddess Nüwa "mother". Seeing this lovely little thing, Nüwa was pleased and named it "human".

Although satisfied, she still thought only one on the earth would be lonely, then she kneaded a lot of clay figurines day and night until all became alive once touched with the earth and yelled her "mother". Those little creatures were all over the earth, sweeping away the loneliness. She continued kneading clay until it became dark. She felt so tired that she fell asleep leaning against a cliff.

The next day, just after daybreak, she got up and went on

the work, expecting these little creatures can spread all over the earth. However, the world was so big that she felt tired and exhausted soon after. Later she came up with an idea: fetching a vine from the cliff, dipping it into the mire with mud, and flicking it before blobs of clay landed everywhere and became living clay figurines. For a while, human beings were all over the earth. These little creatures were divided into male and female to mate freely and produce offspring. Since then, humans descended and developed from generation to generation.

生难字/词注解 | Notes

抟： 把东西揉弄成球形。

Knead: Make something into a ball.

繁衍： 繁殖、衍生，某种生命及生命系统的生育、连接和延续过程。

Reproduce: Breeding and continuation of a certain life and life system.

故事点评 | Story Comment

女娲是人类始祖，为天地注入生灵与生机，她抟土造人的过程，表现了原始先民对人类自身来源的好奇、追索。同时，女娲也被人们称为“大地母神”，象征着爱与仁慈。她一直为人们所敬爱。

Nüwa is the first ancestor of human beings who brought life and vitality to the world. Her creation of mankind with soil represented the primitive men's curiosity to search for the origin of self. Meanwhile, Nüwa, who is respected and esteemed by people of all time, is also regarded as mother goddess of land who represents love and benevolence.

女娲补天

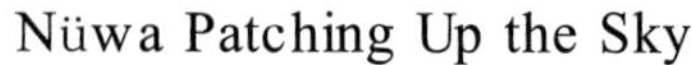

Nüwa Patching Up the Sky

chuán shuō pán gǔ kāi tiān pì dì nǚ wā chuàng zào le rén yǐ hòu
传说盘古开天辟地，女娲创造了人以后，

rén men shì shì dài dài fán yǎn shēng xī guò zhe xìng fú de shēng huó rán
人们世世代代繁衍生息，过着幸福的生活。然

ér yǒu yì nián fā shēng le yí jiàn bú xìng de shì huǒ shén zhù róng hé shuǐ
而，有一年发生了一件不幸的事。火神祝融和水

shén gòng gōng wèi le zhēng duó wáng wèi dǎ qǐ zhàng lái le tā men zài bù
神共工为了争夺王位打起仗来了。他们在不

zhōu shān dà zhàn jiǎo de fēng yún biàn sè hūn tiān hēi dì bǎi xìng bù dé
周山大战，搅得风云变色，昏天黑地，百姓不得

ān níng zhù róng hé gòng gōng cóng tiān tíng yì zhí dǎ dào rén jiān jié guǒ
安宁。祝融和共工从天庭一直打到人间，结果

zhù róng dǎ shèng le dàn shī bài de gòng gōng bù fú qì yí nù zhī xià
祝融打胜了。但失败的共工不服气，一怒之下，
bǎ tóu zhuàng xiàng bù zhōu shān yí shùn jiān bù zhōu shān bēng tā liè kāi
把头撞向不周山。一瞬间，不周山崩塌裂开
le pán gǔ yòng lái chēng kāi tiān dì zhī jiān de dà zhù dōu zhé duàn le tiān
了，盘古用来撑开天地之间的大柱都折断了，天
wāi xié zhe dǎo zài yì biān chū xiàn le yí gè dà kū long dì yě xiàn chéng
歪斜着倒在一边，出现了一个大窟窿，地也陷成
yí dào dào dà liè wén shān lín zhōng rán qǐ le dà huǒ hóng shuǐ cóng dì
一道道大裂纹。山林中燃起了大火，洪水从地
dǐ xià pēn yǒng chū lái rén men zài hóng shuǐ zhōng kū tiān hǎn dì kǔ kǔ
底下喷涌出来，人们在洪水中哭天喊地，苦苦
zhēng zhá nà xiē lóng shé měng shòu yě chèn cǐ jī huì chū lái tūn shí
挣扎，那些龙蛇猛兽也趁此机会出来吞食
rén mìng
人命。

nǚ wā kàn dào le rén lèi de bēi cǎn zāo yù fēi cháng nán guò tā
女娲看到了人类的悲惨遭遇，非常难过。她
wèi le zhěng jiù rén lèi zhōng zhǐ zhè chǎng zāi nàn jué dìng qù cǎi jí shí
为了拯救人类，终止这场灾难，决定去采集石
kuài lái mí bǔ liè kāi dà dòng de tiān tā fān shān yuè lǐng dào chù qù xún
块来弥补裂开大洞的天。她翻山越岭，到处去寻
zhǎo hé shì de dì fang lái bǔ tiān zuì hòu xuǎn zé le dōng hǎi zhī wài de hǎi
找合适的地方来补天，最后选择了东海之外的海
shàng xiān shān tiān tái shān tā bǎ shān shang de wǔ sè shí zuò wéi
上仙山——天台山。她把山上的五色石作为
yuán liào bǎ shān shang de jù shí duī qì zài yì qǐ zuò wéi lú zào bìng qiě
原料，把山上的巨石堆砌在一起作为炉灶，并且
jiè lái tài yáng shén huǒ jīng guò jiǔ tiān jiǔ yè de yě liàn liàn jiù le sān wàn
借来太阳神火，经过九天九夜的冶炼，炼就了三万

duō kuài wǔ sè jù shí jiē zhe yòu jīng guò jiǔ tiān jiǔ yè tā jiāng zhè sān
多块五色巨石。接着又经过九天九夜，她将这三
wàn duō kuài wǔ cǎi shí yí kuài kuài de duī qǐ lái zuì hòu tā zhōng yú bǎ
万多块五彩石一块块地堆起来。最后，她终于把
tiān bǔ hǎo le kě shì què zhǎo bú dào yòng lái zhī chēng tiān de zhù zi yào
天补好了，可是却找不到用来支撑天的柱子。要
shi méi yǒu zhù zi zhī chēng tiān hái shì huì tā xià lai de
是没有柱子支撑，天还是会塌下来的。

nǚ wā hěn wéi nán zěn me bàn ne tā shí fēn zháo jí zhǐ hǎo
女娲很为难。怎么办呢？她十分着急，只好
jiāng bēi fù tiān tái shān de shén guī de sì zhī jiǎo kǎn xià lai zhī chēng qǐ
将背负天台山的神龟的四只脚砍下来支撑起
tiān kě shì tiān tái shān yào shì méi yǒu shén guī de fù zài jiù huì chén rù
天。可是天台山要是没有神龟的负载，就会沉入
hǎi dǐ yú shì nǚ wā jiāng tiān tái shān yí dào dōng hǎi de páng biān qù le
海底。于是女娲将天台山移到东海的旁边去了。
suí hòu nǚ wā hái shā le cán hài rén mín de hēi lóng wèi le néng gòu fáng zhǐ
随后，女娲还杀了残害人民的黑龙。为了能够防止
hóng shuǐ fàn làn nǚ wā hái shōu jí le dà liàng lú cǎo bǎ tā men shāo chéng
洪水泛滥，女娲还收集了大量芦草，把它们烧成
huī sǎ xiàng sì chù yǐ dǔ sè màn yán kāi lái de ní shí liú
灰，洒向四处，以堵塞漫延开来的泥石流。

jīng guò nǚ wā yì fān xīn láo zhěng zhì cāng tiān zǒng suàn bǔ shàng le
经过女娲一番辛劳整治，苍天总算补上了，
tiān dì jiān huī fù le níng jìng dì tián píng le shuǐ zhǐ zhù le lóng shé
天地间恢复了宁静。地填平了，水止住了，龙蛇
měng shòu yě bú jiàn le zōng yǐng rén mín yòu chóng xīn guò shàng le ān lè de
猛兽也不见了踪影，人民又重新过上了安乐的
shēng huó dàn shì zhè chǎng zāi huò yě liú xià le hén jì cóng cǐ tiān
生活。但是，这场灾祸也留下了痕迹。从此天

hái shì yǒu xiē xiàng xī běi qīng xié tài yáng yuè liang hé xīng xing dōu bú zì
还是有些向西北倾斜；太阳、月亮和星星都不自

rán de guī xiàng xī fāng yòu yīn wèi dì xiàng dōng nán tā xiàn suǒ yǐ yí qiè
然地归向西方；又因为地向东南塌陷，所以一切

jiāng hé dōu wǎng nà lǐ bēn liú
江河都往那里奔流。

According to Chinese legend, after Pangu separated the sky and the earth and Nüwa created human, human beings lived a peaceful and happy life. However, one year, a disaster happened. The Fire God Zhurong and the Water God Gonggong fought from the sky to the earth for the throne at the Buzhou Mountain. They stirred the wind and clouds to change their colors and annoyed the common people. They fought from the sky to the earth. Finally Zhurong won the fight while Gonggong was unconvinced of the failure, therefore Gonggong bumped his head into the Buzhou Mountain. In a second, the mountain collapsed, breaking the column used by Pangu to separate the sky and the earth. The sky leaned on one side, making a big hole in the sky and lines of cracks on the land. Fires burned up in the woods. Flood spurted out from underground. People were crying and struggling bitterly in the flood. Those dragons, snakes and beasts also took advantage of the opportunity to devour human beings.

Upon seeing the suffering of human beings, Nüwa felt

distressed and decided to collect stones to patch up the hole in the sky so as to end the disaster. Crossing mountains after mountains, she searched around to find the suitable place for patching. Finally she chose the Tiantai Mountain, a holy mountain, outside the East Sea, where she picked up the stones of five colors as the raw material and piled up giant stones on the mountain into a furnace stove. With the holy fire from the sun, after nine days and nights smelting, she made over thirty thousand giant stones of five colors. Then after another nine days and nights, she piled those giant stones up and finally patched up the sky. But she found that without the column to uphold the sky, the sky would still collapse.

Nüwa was baffled, not knowing what to do. She was so anxious that she chopped down the four feet of the holy turtle who carried the Tiantai Mountain on the back. But without the holy turtle, the Tiantai Mountain would sink into the sea. Then she took it to the place near the East Sea. Later, Nüwa killed the black dragon that devoured the human beings. To stop the flood, she collected large amounts of reeds and burned them into ashes which were spread around to block the mud rock flow.

With great pains and toils, Nüwa finally patched up the sky. Everything was settled. The ground was filled up, the flood was stopped and the dragons, snakes and beasts disappeared. People again lived a happy and peaceful life. But the disaster still left some impacts. Since then, the sky leaned towards the northwest. The sun, the moon and the stars leaned towards the west sky. Moreover, as the earth collapsed towards the southeast, all the rivers and streams were flowing towards there.

故事点评 | Story Comment

女娲补天的故事和女娲造人的故事一样著名,在我国家喻户晓。女娲炼石补天,反映了她拯救人类,为人们开辟和睦安宁生活的伟大精神。后人为了纪念女娲,特意在天台山下建立女娲庙,世代供奉。据说来朝拜的人很多,香火不断。

The story of Nüwa's patching up the sky is as famous as the story of her creating the human beings. Both are household stories. Smelting stones for patching up the sky reflects the great spirit of Nüwa who saved human beings and helped them regain a peaceful and happy life. To commemorate Nüwa, the descendents built Nüwa Temple where lots of people came for worship.

燧人氏钻木取火

Suiren Drilling Wood to Make a Fire

yuǎn gǔ shí qī rén lèi duì huǒ de zuò yòng yì diǎnr dōu bù liǎo
远古时期，人类对火的作用一点儿都不了

jiě rén men chī méi yǒu zhǔ shú de shí wù rěn shòu hán lěng hé hēi yè de
解。人们吃没有煮熟的食物，忍受寒冷和黑夜的

zhé mó dà shén fú xī kàn dào rén jiān bǎi xìng de kǔ nàn fēi cháng nán
折磨。大神伏羲看到人间百姓的苦难，非常难

guò yú shì dà zhǎn shén tōng zài shù lín zhōng jiàng xià yì chǎng léi yǔ
过，于是大展神通，在树林中降下一场雷雨。

suí zhe pā pā de shēng yīn léi diàn pī zài shù mù shang shù mù suí jí
随着“啪啪”的声音，雷电劈在树木上，树木随即

rán shāo qǐ lái hěn kuài jiù shāo chéng le dà huǒ rén men bèi léi diàn hé
燃烧起来，很快就烧成了大火。人们被雷电和

dà huǒ xià huài le dào chù bēn táo
大火吓坏了，到处奔逃。

dào le wǎn shang léi yǔ tíng le yǔ hòu de dà dì shí fēn cháo shī
到了晚上，雷雨停了，雨后的大地十分潮湿
hé yīn lěng táo sàn de rén men yòu chóng xīn huì jù dào le yì qǐ tā men
和阴冷，逃散的人们又重新汇聚到了一起。他们
jīng kǒng de kàn zhe rán shāo de shù mù zhè shí hou yǒu gè nián qīng rén fā
惊恐地看着燃烧的树木，这时候有个年轻人发
xiàn yǐ qián jīng cháng chū xiàn de yě shòu bú jiàn le ér nà xiē bèi shāo sǐ
现，以前经常出现的野兽不见了，而那些被烧死
kǎo jiāo de yě shòu fā chū le zhèn zhèn xiāng wèi rén men gāo xìng de jù
烤焦的野兽，发出了阵阵香味。人们高兴地聚
dào huǒ de páng biān fēn chī shāo guò de yě shòu ròu jué de hǎo chī jí le
到火的旁边，分吃烧过的野兽肉，觉得好吃极了。
zhè shí rén men fā xiàn zhǐ yào yǒu huǒ jiù bú huì hán lěng kǎo shú de ròu bǐ
这时，人们发现只要有火就不会寒冷，烤熟的肉比
shēng ròu gèng jiā měi wèi yóu cǐ tā men gǎn dào le huǒ de zhēn guì yú
生肉更加美味，由此，他们感到了火的珍贵。于
shì tā men jiǎn lái shù zhī bù tíng de tiān jiā dào huǒ duī shàng miàn bú
是，他们拣来树枝，不停地添加到火堆上面，不
ràng huǒ xī miè bìng qiě měi tiān dōu fēn pài rén lái shǒu hù huǒ zhǒng kě
让火熄灭，并且，每天都分派人来守护火种。可
shì yǒu yì tiān zhí shǒu de rén shuì zháo le huǒ xī miè le rén men chóng
是有一天，值守的人睡着了，火熄灭了，人们重
xīn xiàn rù le hēi àn hé hán lěng zhī zhōng
新陷入了黑暗和寒冷之中。

fú xī yì xīn xiǎng bāng zhù shòu kǔ de rén men tā tuō mèng gěi nà
伏羲一心想帮助受苦的人们，他托梦给那
ge nián qīng rén gào su tā zài yáo yuǎn de xī fāng yǒu gè suì míng guó
个年轻人，告诉他："在遥远的西方有个燧明国，

那里有火种，你可以去那里把火种取回来。”年轻人醒了，想起梦里大神说的话，决心到燧明国去寻找火种。年轻人翻山越岭，历尽艰辛，终于来到了燧明国。可是这里没有阳光，不分昼夜，四处一片黑暗，根本没有火。年轻人非常失望，就坐在一棵大树下休息。

突然，年轻人眼前有亮光一闪，又一闪，把周围照得很明亮。年轻人立刻站起来，四处寻找光源。这时候他发现就在这棵树上，有几只大鸟正在用短而硬的喙不停地啄食树上的虫子。只要它们一啄，树上就闪出明亮的火花。年轻人看到这种情景，才恍然大悟。他找来各种树枝，耐心地用不同的树枝在树干上面进行刮擦。终于，树枝上冒起烟，擦出火花来了。年轻人高兴地流下了眼泪。

hòu lái niánqīng rén huí dào le jiā xiāng wèi rén men dài lái le yǒng
后来，年轻人回到了家乡，为人们带来了永
yuǎn bú huì xī miè de huǒ zhǒng jí zuān mù qǔ huǒ de bàn fǎ
远不会熄灭的火种，即“钻木取火”的办法。
cóng nà yǐ hòu rén men zài yě bú yòng shēng huó zài hán lěng hé kǒng jù
从那以后，人们再也不用生活在寒冷和恐惧
zhōng le
中了。

In ancient times, human knew nothing about fire. They had uncooked food, suffered coldness and bore darkness. The god Fuxi exhibited supernatural power to make a thunderstorm fall in the woods after seeing the sorrowful scene on the earth. The thunder and lightning hit the branches, accompanied with big sounds, and woods burned up. In a while, the fire became a big one. Freaked out by the thunderstorm and fire, people fled away.

When night came, the thunderstorm stopped. It was wet and cold. The fleeing people came together again and stared at the burning woods in horror. At that time, a young man found the beasts always hanging around were no longer there and the roasted beasts smelled good. People came together by the fire gladly and shared the delicious meat contentedly. All of them agreed the meat tasted good. Moreover, people found they would not feel cold once with fire and the cooked food was more delicious than the raw one. They realized the preciousness and importance of fire, so they collected branches and assigned people to protect the fire every day. But one day, the person on duty fell asleep, and the fire burnt out. People were in darkness and coldness again.

Fuxi set on helping those suffering people, so he appeared in the young man's dream and told him to go to the distant Suiming Country to fetch the fire back. After he woke up, the young man determined to go to search for the fire according to the indication of god appearing in his dream. Crossing mountains after mountains and going through all kinds of hardships, he eventually arrived in Suiming Country. But there was no light, no day or night, no fire but only darkness left. There was no fire. The young man felt overwhelmingly disappointed to rest under a tall tree.

All of a sudden, there appeared a flash that lighted the surroundings up. Instantly the young man stood up and began to search for the light around. Then he found it was in the tree where several birds were pecking on the trunk with their short and sharp beaks. The place they pecked on would spark brightly. It occurred to him it may be the way of making fire. He collected all kinds of branches and tried to rub them one by one with the trunk patiently. Finally the branch was lighted up and sparked lightly. The young man wept with joy.

Later, he returned home with the fire which would never die out once made by drilling woods. Since then, people would never live in coldness and horror.

生难字/词注解 | Notes

燧：上古取火的器具。

Flint: A piece of tool that is used to produce spark in ancient times.

伏羲：中国古代神话人物。

Fuxi: A character in ancient Chinese myths.

故事点评 | Story Comment

故事中的年轻人百折不挠探索取火的方法，后人为他的勇气和智慧所折服，称他为“燧人”，也就是“取火者”的意思。这个故事展现原始先民从自然中学习生存技能、勇于改造自然的积极进取精神。

The brave young man in the story who searched for fire dauntlessly is admired and respected by the descendants for his remarkable courage and wisdom. People call him “Suiren”, i.e. the person who fetched the fire. The story embodies the enterprising spirit of primitive men who dared to transform nature and learn survival skills from nature.

年的来历

The Origin of "Nian"

xiāng chuán gǔ shí hou yǒu yì zhǒng míng jiào nián de guài shòu tóu
相传古时候有一种名叫"年"的怪兽，头
shang zhǎng zhe jiān ruì de jiǎo fēi cháng xiōng měng nián shòu cháng nián
上长着尖锐的角，非常凶猛。"年"兽长年
jū zhù zài hǎi dǐ měi dào chú xī jiù pá shàng àn lái tūn shí shēng chù shāng
居住在海底，每到除夕就爬上岸来吞食牲畜、伤
hài rén mìng rén men bù dé bù duǒ jìn shān lín zhōng
害人命，人们不得不躲进山林中。

yòu shì yì nián de chú xī wèi le duǒ bì nián shòu de qīn hài rén
又是一年的除夕，为了躲避"年"兽的侵害，人
men xiàng wǎng nián yí yàng táo wǎng shān lín jiù zài rén men zhǔn bèi táo zǒu
们像往年一样逃往山林。就在人们准备逃走

de shí hou yí gè mǎn tóu bái fà de lǎo rén chū xiàn le rén men dōu zài
的时候，一个满头白发的老人出现了。人们都在
máng zhe guān chuāng suǒ mén shōu shi xíng zhuāng méi yǒu shéi zhù yì dào zhè
忙着关窗锁门，收拾行装，没有谁注意到这
wèi lǎo rén zhǐ yǒu cūn tóu de yí wèi lǎo nǎi nai tā hǎo xīn de sòng gěi le
位老人。只有村头的一位老奶奶，她好心地送给了
lǎo rén yì xiē shí wù bìng quàn tā gǎn kuài shàng shān duǒ bì nián shòu
老人一些食物，并劝他赶快上山躲避“年”兽。
shéi zhī nà lǎo rén què xiào dào nín ruò ràng wǒ zài nín jiā lǐ zhù yì wǎn
谁知那老人却笑道：“您若让我在您家里住一晚
shang wǒ yí dìng bǎ nián shòu gǎn zǒu lǎo nǎi nai fēi cháng jīng yà
上，我一定把‘年’兽赶走。”老奶奶非常惊讶，
kě hái shì bù gǎn xiāng xìn tā réng rán jì xù quàn shuō lǎo rén gǎn jǐn lí
可还是不敢相信，她仍然继续劝说老人赶紧离
kāi nà ge lǎo rén zhǐ shì xiào xiao zài yě bù shuō huà le lǎo nǎi nai
开。那个老人只是笑笑，再也不说话了。老奶奶
méi yǒu bàn fǎ zhī hǎo hé dà jiā yì qǐ shàng shān bì nàn qù le
没有办法，只好和大家一起上山避难去了。

dào le bàn yè de shí hou nián shòu chuǎng jìn cūn zhuāng tā fā
到了半夜的时候，“年”兽闯进村庄。它发
xiàn cūn lǐ de qì fēn yǔ wǎng nián bù tóng dào chù shì hēi hū hū de wéi
现村里的气氛与往年不同，到处是黑乎乎的，唯
dú cūn tóu lǎo nǎi nai jiā mén shang tiē zhe dà hóng zhǐ wū zi lǐ liàng zhe
独村头老奶奶家，门上贴着大红纸，屋子里亮着
dēng dēng guāng zài qī hēi de yè lǐ xiǎn de tè bié yào yǎn nián shòu
灯，灯光在漆黑的夜里显得特别耀眼。“年”兽
hún shēn yì dǒu guài jiào le yì shēng hǒu jiào zhe pū xiàng lǎo nǎi nai de fáng
浑身一抖，怪叫了一声，吼叫着扑向老奶奶的房
zi kě shì kuài yào dào mén kǒu de shí hou yuàn zi lǐ tū rán chuán lái
子。可是，快要到门口的时候，院子里突然传来

pēng pēng pā pā de zhà xiǎng shēng nián shòu hún shēn zhàn lì zài
“砰砰”“啪啪”的炸响声，“年”兽浑身战栗，再
bù gǎn wǎng qián měng pū le zhè shí lǎo nǎi nai jiā de mén bèi dǎ kāi
不敢往前猛扑了。这时，老奶奶家的门被打开
le zhǐ jiàn yí wèi shēn pī hóng páo de lǎo rén zhàn zài yuàn nèi hā hā dà
了，只见一位身披红袍的老人站在院内哈哈大
xiào nián shòu shí fēn jīng kǒng gǎn jǐn táo pǎo le yuán lái nián
笑。“年”兽十分惊恐，赶紧逃跑了。原来，“年”
shòu zuì hài pà hóng sè huǒ guāng hé zhà xiǎng
兽最害怕红色、火光和炸响。

dì èr tiān shì zhēng yuè chū yī rén men huí dào jiā fā xiàn cūn lǐ hěn
第二天是正月初一，人们回到家发现村里很
píng ān shí fēn jīng qí zhè shí lǎo nǎi nai cái huǎng rán dà wù gǎn máng
平安，十分惊奇。这时，老奶奶才恍然大悟，赶忙
xiàng xiāng qīn men shuō le nà ge bái tóu fa lǎo rén de shì qing dà jiā zǒu
向乡亲们说了那个白头发老人的事情。大家走
dào lǎo nǎi nai jiā kàn jiàn lǎo nǎi nai jiā mén shang tiē zhe hóng zhǐ yuàn zi
到老奶奶家，看见老奶奶家门上贴着红纸，院子
lǐ yì duī méi yǒu rán shāo wán de zhú zi réng zài pā pā zhà xiǎng wū zi
里一堆没有燃烧完的竹子仍在“啪啪”炸响，屋子
lǐ hái diǎn zhe jǐ gēn hóng là zhú dà jiā kāi xīn jí le zhè jiàn shì hěn
里还点着几根红蜡烛。大家开心极了。这件事很
kuài zài zhōu wéi cūn lǐ chuán kāi le rén men dōu zhī dào le qū gǎn nián
快在周围村里传开了，人们都知道了驱赶“年”
shòu de bàn fǎ
兽的办法。

cóng cǐ měi nián chú xī jiā jiā hù hù dōu tiē hóng duì lián rán fàng
从此，每年除夕，家家户户都贴红对联，燃放
bào zhú zhěng gè wǎn shang dōu dēng huǒ tōng míng quán jiā rén zuò zài yì
爆竹，整个晚上都灯火通明。全家人坐在一

qǐ děng dài xīn nián zhōng shēng qiāo xiǎng de nà yí kè cóng cǐ zhè yì
起，等待新年钟声敲响的那一刻。从此，这一

fēng sú liú chuán de yuè lái yuè guǎng chéng le zhōng huá mín zú zuì lóng zhòng
风俗流传得越来越广，成了中华民族最隆重

de chuán tǒng guò nián
的传统：过年。

According to Chinese legend, in ancient times, there was a savage monster, Nian, with sharp horns on the head. It hid in the sea all year round, only climbing up the shore to devour livestock on every New Year's Eve, which threatened human's life. People had to flee to the mountains for refuge.

Another New Year's Eve came, people were about to flee away as usual when a white haired old man appeared. As people were busy in locking windows and doors, packing food and clothes, nobody noticed the coming of the old man. Only an old woman gave some food to the old man and persuaded him to flee to the mountains with them. But the old man smiled and asked whether he could stay one night in her house and claimed he would drive the monster Nian away. The old woman was shocked but dared not believe him. She insisted on asking the old man to run away while the latter only smiled without saying anything more. Then the old woman fled away with the rest to the mountains.

In the midnight, the monster Nian came to the village and felt something unusual. Everywhere was dark, only the door of the old woman's house was posted with red paper and the light in the old woman's house was on, shining brightly in the dark. The monster Nian trembled, roared, and jumped to the door. But when it came near the door, from the yard came loud and rumbling sound. The monster Nian trembled fiercely and dared not go on moving. Then the door was opened and inside stood a laughing old man in red. The monster Nian was frightened and fled away. It turned out that the monster Nian feared redness, flame and blast.

The next day, it was the first day of the first lunar month when people who sought refuge came back home and were surprised to find the village in safety. They all felt puzzled. Then the old woman came to realize the truth and told the story of the white haired old man to others. They all came to the old woman's house, seeing the doors were posted with red paper and in the yard, some firecrackers were still going off, and several red candles were still lighted in the house. Everyone felt happy. The story was soon spread around so that everyone knew the way of driving the monster Nian away.

Since then, when the annual New Year's Eve came, families would paste red couplets and set off firecrackers. Candles in each household would be lighted brightly all night and the family members would come together waiting for the coming of New Year. This custom spread more and more widely and eventually became the grandest Chinese traditional festival: Spring Festival.

生难字/词注解 | Notes

怪兽：长相怪异的猛兽。

Monster: A strange creature that is very large, ugly and frightening.

除夕：农历一年最后一天的晚上。

The New Year's Eve: The last night of a lunar year.

爆竹：古时用火烧竹，毕剥有声，火花迸裂，称为爆竹。今人用纸卷火药，点燃发响，也称"爆仗"。

Firecracker: In ancient times, people used fire to burn bamboo, which caused a cracking sound and was called "firecracker". Nowadays, people wrap gunpowder in paper which is lightened for the loud sound, and is called "explosive battle".

故事点评 | Story Comment

驱赶年兽的故事，隐喻除旧布新、迎春接福的意义。后来成为中国传统节日：过年。它象征着团圆、幸福、兴旺，寄予人们对新的一年的美好祝愿。

The story of driving Nian away is a metaphor for getting rid of old things and welcoming the new, and wishing the New Year would bring good fortune. Later, it became a Chinese traditional festival: Spring Festival which symbolizes reunion, happiness, luck and people's best wishes for the coming new year.

十二生肖的传说

The 12 Animals of the Chinese Zodiac

chuán shuō yù huáng dà dì xiǎng xuǎn chū shí èr zhǒng dòng wù zuò wéi
传说玉皇大帝想选出十二种动物作为
shēng xiào bìng dìng xià shí jiān ràng dòng wù men lái tiān gōng cān jiā jìng xuǎn dà
生肖，并定下时间让动物们来天宫参加竞选大
huì nà shí māo hé lǎo shǔ shì hǎo péng you suī rán māo bǐ jiào lǎn zǒng
会。那时猫和老鼠是好朋友。虽然猫比较懒，总
shì shuì lǎn jiào dàn shì tā yě xiǎng chéng wéi shēng xiào zhōng de yì yuán
是睡懒觉，但是它也想成为生肖中的一员。
suǒ yǐ jiù zhǔ fù lǎo shǔ qù de shí hou jì dé jiào shàng tā kě shì lǎo shǔ
所以就嘱咐老鼠去的时候记得叫上它。可是老鼠
wàng jì le lǎo shǔ xiān qù zhǎo lǎo niú shuō lǎo niú qǐ de zǎo pǎo de
忘记了。老鼠先去找老牛，说老牛起得早跑得

kuài jiào lǎo niú dài shàng tā nà shí de lóng méi yǒu jī jiao jī yǒu jī
快，叫老牛带上它。那时的龙没有犄角，鸡有犄
jiao lóng jiù xiàng jī jiè le jī jiao
角，龙就向鸡借了犄角。

yù dìng de shí rì dào le chú le māo hái zài shuì jiào wài qí tā dòng
预定的时日到了，除了猫还在睡觉外，其他动
wù dōu zhēng xiān kǒng hòu gǎn wǎng tiān gōng lǎo shǔ zuò zài niú bèi shang
物都争先恐后赶往天宫。老鼠坐在牛背上，
dào dá tiān tíng hòu lǎo shǔ cēng de yí xià tiào dào le zuì qián miàn yù
到达天庭后，老鼠“噌”的一下跳到了最前面，玉
huáng dà dì bǎ tā pái zài dì yī lǎo niú pái dì èr lǎo hǔ suí hòu dào
皇大帝把它排在第一，老牛排第二；老虎随后到
le pái dì sān jiē zhe shì tù zi pái dì sì lóng pái dì wǔ shé zhǎng
了，排第三；接着是兔子，排第四；龙排第五，蛇长
de xiàng lóng yú shì pái dì liù mǎ hé yáng yě dào le yù huáng dà dì
得像龙，于是排第六；马和羊也到了，玉皇大帝
jiù ràng tā men pái dì qī dì bā hóu zi běn lái pái sān shí duō wèi kě
就让它们排第七、第八；猴子本来排三十多位，可
shì tā lā zhe tiān shàng de yún duǒ fēi pǎo tiào dào le qián miàn pái dì jiǔ
是它拉着天上的云朵飞跑，跳到了前面，排第九；
jiē zhe jī gǒu zhū yě fēn fēn bèi xuǎn shàng
接着鸡、狗、猪也纷纷被选上。

shí èr shēng xiào què dìng hǎo le māo cái xǐng lái tā hěn shēng qì
十二生肖确定好了，猫才醒来。它很生气，
děng lǎo shǔ huí jiā shí māo jiù yào zhuī zhe qù yǎo tā ér lóng lái dào dà
等老鼠回家时，猫就要追着去咬它。而龙来到大
hǎi biān kàn dào yǒu jī jiao hòu gèng piào liang le jiù méi yǒu bǎ jī jiao huán
海边，看到有犄角后更漂亮了，就没有把犄角还
gěi jī cóng cǐ jī duì lóng tè bié de yuàn hèn
给鸡。从此，鸡对龙特别地怨恨。

According to Chinese legend，the Emperor of Heaven wanted to select 12 animals to be the zodiac and set a time for animals to compete in the heavenly palace. At that time，cat and rat were good friends. Cat liked sleeping but also wanted to be selected，so he asked rat to take him along to the contest. But rat forgot to call on cat, instead he invited ox to go with him，considering ox usually got up early and ran fast. At that time，dragon had no horns. It borrowed horns from rooster.

The scheduled day came. Apart from the sleeping cat，other animals all rushed to the fore and hurried to the heavenly palace. Rat sat on the back of ox. As soon as they were close to the heavenly palace，rat jumped to the front suddenly and was ranked the first followed by ox. Tiger came closely after ox and was ranked the third by the Emperor of Heaven. The following one was rabbit who ranked the fourth; dragon was the fifth. As snake looked like dragon，it went to the sixth，followed with horse and sheep ranking the seventh and eighth respectively. Monkey was in a position after 30th at first，but he ran quickly with the cloud and eventually jumped to the ninth. Then rooster，dog and boar were all selected.

The members of the zodiac had already been set before cat woke up. When rat returned home，cat chased rat and bit it furiously. While dragon came by the sea，finding him to be more attractive with horns，he was not willing to return the horns back to rooster. Since then，rooster resented dragon particularly.

生难字/词注解 | Notes

生肖：也称属相(shǔ xiàng)，是中国和东亚地区的一些民族用来代表年份和人的出生年的十二种动物，统称十二生肖或十二属相。

Zodiac：In China and some nations in East Asia，the twelve animals，representing the twelve Earthly Branches，are used to symbolize the year in which a person was born.

犄角：牛、羊、鹿等头上长出的坚硬的尖东西。

Horn：A hard pointed part that grows，usually in pairs，on the heads of some animals，such as cows，sheep，and deer.

故事点评 | Story Comment

十二生肖是中国民间计算年龄的方法，也是一种古老的纪年法。生肖的循环周期为十二年，每一个人在出生年都有一种动物作为生肖，即鼠、牛、虎、兔、龙、蛇、马、羊、猴、鸡、狗、猪，展现出中华人民丰富的想象力和创造力。

The 12 Animals of the Chinese Zodiac，a Chinese folk method for calculating age，is an old chronological way of recording years by which the years are designated. Zodiac runs in a 12-year cycle，each year of which is named after one animal: rat，ox，tiger，rabbit，dragon，snake，horse，sheep，monkey，rooster，dog，boar，which shows Chinese people's rich imagination and creativity.

神农尝百草

Shennong Discovering the Curative Virtues of Plants

yuǎn gǔ shí hou rén men bù zhī dào yào wù de gōng yòng shēng bìng
远古时候，人们不知道药物的功用，生病

hòu dé bú dào yī zhì shén nóng hěn tóng qíng rén men de zāo yù tā jué xīn
后得不到医治。神农很同情人们的遭遇，他决心

cháng shì gè lèi huā cǎo xún zhǎo dào zhì bìng jiù rén de yào fāng
尝试各类花草，寻找到治病救人的药方。

yǒu yì tiān shén nóng de nǚ ér huā ruǐ gōng zhǔ dé le zhòng bìng
有一天，神农的女儿花蕊公主得了重病，

shén nóng jiāng jǐ zhǒng huā cǎo hùn zài yì qǐ pèi chéng le cǎo yào ràng tā
神农将几种花草混在一起，配成了草药让她

fú xià jié guǒ huā ruǐ gōng zhǔ de bìng hǎo le hái shēng xià lái yì zhī
服下。结果花蕊公主的病好了，还生下来一只

xiǎo niǎo shén nóng gěi tā qǔ míng wéi huā ruǐ niǎo zhè zhī xiǎo niǎo hún
小鸟，神农给它取名为“花蕊鸟”。这只小鸟浑
shēn cuì lǜ tòu míng tōng rén xìng shén nóng bǎ huā ruǐ gōng zhǔ chī guò
身翠绿、透明，通人性。神农把花蕊公主吃过
de yào fēn kāi zài guō lǐ áo rán hòu jiāng yào shuǐ wèi gěi xiǎo niǎo guān
的药分开在锅里熬，然后将药水喂给小鸟，观
chá yào shuǐ zài xiǎo niǎo dù cháng zhōng de biàn huà yào wèi wán le shén
察药水在小鸟肚肠中的变化。药喂完了，神
nóng fā xiàn yào shuǐ zài xiǎo niǎo shēn tǐ lǐ jīng guò sān yīn sān yáng shí èr
农发现药水在小鸟身体里经过三阴三阳十二
jīng mài
经脉。

cóng cǐ shén nóng dài zhe zhè zhī niǎo fān shān yuè lǐng cǎi zhāi gè zhǒng
从此，神农带着这只鸟翻山越岭采摘各种
cǎo gēn shù pí zhǒng zi guǒ shí bǔ zhuō gè zhǒng fēi qín zǒu shòu yú
草根、树皮、种子、果实；捕捉各种飞禽走兽、鱼
biē xiā chóng wā jué gè zhǒng shí tou rán hòu yī yī áo zhǔ ràng xiǎo niǎo
鳖虾虫；挖掘各种石头；然后一一熬煮，让小鸟
cháng shì guān chá yào yè zài tā shēn tǐ lǐ de biàn huà qíng kuàng guò le
尝试，观察药液在它身体里的变化情况。过了
hěn cháng yí duàn shí jiān shén nóng zhōng yú huì zhì chū rén tǐ de shí èr jīng
很长一段时间，神农终于绘制出人体的十二经
mài tú bìng zhuàn xiě běn cǎo jīng yì shū
脉图，并撰写《本草经》一书。

zhī hòu shén nóng jì xù dài zhe zhè zhī niǎo sì chù xíng zǒu tàn fǎng
之后，神农继续带着这只鸟四处行走探访。
yì tiān tā lái dào tài háng shān de xiǎo běi dǐng zhuō le yì zhī chóng zi wèi
一天，他来到太行山的小北顶，捉了一只虫子喂
xiǎo niǎo méi xiǎng dào zhè zhī chóng zi dú qì tài dà yǐ zhì yú bǎ xiǎo niǎo
小鸟，没想到这只虫子毒气太大，以至于把小鸟

dú sǐ le shén nóng hěn bēi shāng tā fǎng zhào xiǎo niǎo de mú yàng diāo kè
毒死了。神农很悲伤，他仿照小鸟的模样雕刻

le yì zhī mù tou niǎo suí shēn xié dài zhe jì xù wèi rén liáo shāng zhì bìng
了一只木头鸟，随身携带着，继续为人疗伤治病。

hòu lái shén nóng zài xiǎo běi dǐng liǎng biān de bǎi cǎo wā wù cháng le
后来，神农在小北顶两边的百草洼，误尝了

duàn cháng cǎo bú xìng shì shì
断肠草，不幸逝世。

In ancient times, people knew nothing about the medical use of herbal plants. If they got ill, they could not get medical care. Shennong felt sympathy for people and decided to taste all kinds of plants to search for the curative herbs.

One day, the daughter of Shennong, Princess Huarui, was ill. After she had the medicinal herbs mixed with several plants made by her father, she was totally cured and even gave birth to a bird. Shennong named the transparent bird Huarui which was an emerald green colored bird with the thinking ability like humans'. Shennong boiled the medicinal herbs both for Princess Huarui and the bird Huarui. The latter was fed the drug and was observed the changes in its intestines. Shennong found the drug run through its three *yin* and three *yang* as well as twelve channels.

Since then, with the bird's help, Shennong picked all kinds of grass roots, barks, seeds and fruits, caught various types of birds

and beasts, fish, turtles, shrimps, insects and worms, dug different kinds of stones, boiled them and let the bird have a try to see what would happen in its body. After a long time, Shennong finally drew out the twelve channels of human and wrote a book named *Herbal Classic*.

Later, he travelled to the North Top of the Taihang Mountain where he found a worm and fed it to the bird. Unexpectedly, this worm was so poisonous that it poisoned the bird to death. Sorrowful and grieved, Shennong made a wooden bird similar to the bird's image, carrying it along with him. He went on healing and curing patients. Later, in the low-lying side of the North Top, the tasting of gelsemium elegans put him to death.

生难字/词注解 | Notes

花蕊: 花的雌性繁殖器官。 此处特指人(鸟)名。

Huarui (Pistil): The female organs of a flower, which receive the pollen and produce seeds. Here it refers to the name of a person/bird.

熬: 把食物等放在水里煮。

Boil: Cook the food in water.

鳖: 爬行动物,形状似龟。

Bie (Trionyx sinensis): A soft-shelled turtle.

故事点评 | Story Comment

神农为了寻找治病救人的药方，不惜冒着生命危险品尝各种草药，他对生命的悲悯和博爱精神让后人景仰。为了纪念他，后人把小北顶改名为“神农坛”，并在神农坛上修建神农庙和神农塑像，以示敬奉。

To find the curative herbs for curing patients, Shennong tasted all kinds of herbs at the risk of life. His sympathy for people and his humanity spirit are respected by the later generations. People renamed the North Top as Shennong Altar and built Shennong Temple and a Shennong statue for pious worship.

仓颉造字

Cangjie Inventing Chinese Characters

chuán shuō cāng jié shì huáng dì de yì yuán dà chén fù zé guǎn lǐ
传说仓颉是黄帝的一员大臣，负责管理
shēng kǒu shí wù děng zhàng mù cāng jié rén hěn cōng míng zuò shì hěn xì
牲口、食物等账目。仓颉人很聪明，做事很细
xīn hěn kuài jiù jì zhù le suǒ yǒu shēng kǒu hé shí wù de shù liàng dàn
心，很快就记住了所有牲口和食物的数量。但
shì suí zhe shēng kǒu shí wù de shù liàng zài zhú jiàn zēng dà biàn huà dāng
是，随着牲口、食物的数量在逐渐增大、变化，当
shí méi yǒu wén zì gèng méi yǒu zhǐ hé bǐ suǒ yǐ dān dú píng jiè tóu nǎo
时没有文字，更没有纸和笔，所以，单独凭借头脑
jì yì fēi cháng kùn nan zěn me bàn ne
记忆非常困难。怎么办呢？

cāng jié xiǎng ya xiǎng ya xiān shì xiǎng dào yòng gè zhǒng bù tóng yán
仓颉想呀想呀，先是想到用各种不同颜

sè de shéng zi dǎ chéng jié biǎo shì gè zhǒng bù tóng de shēng kǒu shí
色的绳子打成结，表示各种不同的牲口、食
wù dàn shí jiān yì cháng jiǔ jiù bú zòu xiào le zhè zēng jiā de shù mù
物。但时间一长久，就不奏效了。这增加的数目
zài shéng zi shang dǎ gè jié hěn fāng biàn ér jiǎn shǎo shù mù shí yào jiāng
在绳子上打个结很方便，而减少数目时，要将
shéng zi shang de jié jiě kāi jiù tè bié má fan le cāng jié yòu xiǎng dào
绳子上的结解开就特别麻烦了。仓颉又想到
le zài shéng zi shang dǎ quān quan zài quān zi lǐ guà shang gè shì gè yàng
了在绳子上打圈圈，在圈子里挂上各式各样
de bèi ké lái dài tì tā suǒ guǎn lǐ de dōng xi zēng jiā le jiù tiān yí
的贝壳，来代替他所管理的东西。增加了就添一
gè bèi ké jiǎn shǎo le jiù qù diào yí gè bèi ké zhè zhǒng bàn fǎ guǒ rán
个贝壳，减少了就去掉一个贝壳。这种办法果然
tǐng yǒu xiào yì lián yòng le hǎo duō nián huáng dì jiàn cāng jié zhè yàng néng
挺有效，一连用了好多年。黄帝见仓颉这样能
gàn jiào tā guǎn lǐ de shì qing jiù yuè lái yuè duō dàn duì yú jù dà de
干，叫他管理的事情就越来越多。但对于巨大的
shù mù cāng jié yǐ qián de fāng fǎ jiù bù qǐ zuò yòng le tā yīn cǐ hěn
数目，仓颉以前的方法就不起作用了。他因此很
kǔ nǎo
苦恼。

yì tiān tā cān jiā gōng tíng lǐ de dà xíng wéi liè huó dòng tā qí
一天，他参加宫廷里的大型围猎活动。他骑
zhe mǎ zǒu zài lù shang zǒu dào yí gè fēn chà lù kǒu shí kàn dào jǐ gè lǎo
着马走在路上，走到一个分岔路口时，看到几个老
rén wèi zǒu nǎ tiáo lù ér zhēng biàn yí gè lǎo rén yào wǎng dōng shuō nà
人为走哪条路而争辩。一个老人要往东，说那
biān yǒu líng yáng yí gè lǎo rén yào wǎng běi shuō qián miàn yǒu lù qún yí
边有羚羊；一个老人要往北，说前面有鹿群；一

gè lǎo rén yào wǎng xī shuō yǒu liǎng zhī lǎo hǔ bù jí shí dǎ sǐ jiù huì
个老人要往西，说有两只老虎，不及时打死，就会
cuò guò jī huì cāng jié jīng guò xún wèn cái zhī dào yuán lái zhè jǐ gè lǎo
错过机会。仓颉经过询问才知道，原来这几个老
rén dōu shì kàn zhe dì shang yě shòu de tí yìn lái pàn duàn de cāng jié shòu
人都是看着地上野兽的蹄印来判断的。仓颉受
dào qǐ fā tā xīn xiǎng jì rán yí gè jiǎo yìn dài biǎo yì zhǒng yě shòu
到启发，他心想，既然一个脚印代表一种野兽，
nà me wǒ yě kě yǐ yòng fú hào lái biǎo shì wù pǐn de shù mù ya tā
那么，我也可以用符号来表示物品的数目呀。他
huí jiā zhī hòu kāi shǐ yòng gè zhǒng fú hào lái jì zǎi wù pǐn de shù liàng
回家之后，开始用各种符号来记载物品的数量。
guǒ rán tā bǎ zhàng mù guǎn lǐ de hěn yǒu tiáo lǐ
果然，他把账目管理得很有条理。

huáng dì zhī dào hòu duì cǐ dà jiā zàn shǎng wěi pài cāng jié dào
黄帝知道后，对此大加赞赏，委派仓颉到
gè gè bù luò qù chuán shòu zhè zhǒng fāng fǎ jiàn jiàn de zhè xiē fú hào
各个部落去传授这种方法。渐渐地，这些符号
de yòng fǎ tuī guǎng kāi le zhè zhǒng yòng lái dài biǎo shì wù yì yì de
的用法推广开了。这种用来代表事物意义的
fú hào jí zuì yuán shǐ de xiàng xíng wén zì zhú jiàn yǎn biàn chéng jīn tiān
符号，即最原始的象形文字，逐渐演变成今天
tōng yòng de hàn zì cāng jié yīn cǐ bèi hòu rén zūn chēng wéi zào zì
通用的汉字。仓颉因此被后人尊称为“造字
shèng rén
圣人”。

According to Chinese legend, Cangjie was an officer working for Emperor Huang, in charge of the accounts of animals and food. Being smart and careful, it took just a little time for him to remember the number of animals and food. But as the number increased, the task would become rather difficult when there were no written words, paper or pens for use but human's memory to be relied on. How to solve the problem?

Cangjie thought over and over again to find a way to tackle the problem. Firstly he knotted different colored strings to show the different numbers of animals and food. But it didn't last long because making a knot would be easy and convenient, while the number decreased, it would become troublesome to unlock the knot. Then he attached shells to the looped strings to show numbers. An added shell could stand for a new item. This method was effective and useful which was used for several years. Because of his capability, Emperor Huang gave him more and more stuff to take charge of. But he felt helpless to large numbers which troubled him greatly.

One day, he joined a grand hunting activity. Riding a horse on a muddy road, he saw several old men arguing about which road to take at a junction. An old man said they should go to the east where there might be antelopes. Another old man insisted on going to the north where there might be deer. One old man said they should go to the west or they would miss the opportunity to beat the two tigers there. After talking with those old men, Cangjie realized they got the clue from the hoof prints of beasts on the ground. Cangjie was inspired to know that each hoof print could stand for one type of beast, and then he could use different symbols to show different numbers so as to manage and record the amount of food and animals. After he returned home, he began to create the way of using different symbols to show different things. In this way, he finally could manage things in order.

After learning his story, Emperor Huang highly appreciated and praised him, ordering him to impart this way to each tribe. Gradually, these symbols became popular. One symbol standing for a certain matter is the most original pictograph which altogether have evolved into today's Chinese characters. Hence, Cangjie was honored as Word-making Saint.

生难字/词注解 | Notes

仓颉： 传说中造字的史官。

Cangjie: Word-making historiographer.

圈圈： 圆圈。

Loop: Circle.

蹄印： 马、牛、羊等的脚印。

Hoof print: An animal's foot mark left on a surface, like horse, cattle, sheep, etc.

赞赏： 高度评价。

Appreciate and praise: Highly comment.

故事点评 | Story Comment

仓颉用符号来表示事物的意义,形成最原始的象形文字,它结束了远古时期结绳记事的蒙昧时代,为汉字的形成做出巨大贡献,因而被尊称为"字圣"。他的故事告诉我们,一切经验都源于不断地亲身实践,一切科学的发明都源于不懈地尝试与艰辛的努力,只有在长期积累、总结、实践中才能创造奇迹。

Cangjie used symbols to show the meanings of things, which formed the most original pictographs. It ended the barbaric age of recording by knots in ancient times. Since he made great contribution to the formation of Chinese characters, he is honored as Word-making Saint. His story tells us: all experience come from continual personal practice, all scientific inventions come from striving attempts and great efforts. Only with long-time accumulation, summarizing and practice can the miracles occur.

伏羲伐桐制瑶琴

Fuxi Cutting Phoenix Tree to Make Peptachord

chuán shuō fú xī shì tiān shén de hái zi tā de mǔ qīn huá xū shì yīn
传说伏羲是天神的孩子，她的母亲华胥氏因

wèi shuāng jiǎo cǎi dào le yì zhī yóu tiān shén liú xià de jiǎo yìn hòu lái jiù huái
为双脚踩到了一只由天神留下的脚印，后来就怀

yùn shēng xià le fú xī yīn ér fú xī yì chū shēng jiù jù yǒu le gāo
孕，生下了伏羲。因而，伏羲一出生就具有了高

chāo de shén lì zhǎng dà hòu fú xī jiè zhù shén lì zài dōng fāng jiàn lì
超的神力。长大后伏羲借助神力，在东方建立

le zì jǐ de wáng guó fú xī shí shí chá kàn rén jiān lǚ xíng tiān dì jiào
了自己的王国。伏羲时时察看人间，履行天帝教

huì mín zhòng de zhí zé tā bǎ huǒ zhǒng dài gěi rén men shǐ rén men gǎi
诲民众的职责。他把火种带给人们，使人们改

biàn chī shēng shí de xí guàn tā mó fǎng zhī zhū jié wǎng de yàng zi biān
变吃生食的习惯；他模仿蜘蛛结网的样子，编

zhī yú wǎng jiāo huì rén men bǔ yú fú xī jiù zhè yàng bú duàn de gěi rén
织鱼网，教会人们捕鱼。伏羲就这样不断地给人
men zào fú
们造福。

hòu lái fú xī kàn dào rén jiān de shēng huó tài dān diào chén mèn le
后来，伏羲看到人间的生活太单调沉闷了，
jiù xiǎng chuàng zào chū yì zhǒng kě yǐ yǎn zòu de yuè qì gěi rén jiān de
就想创造出一种可以演奏的乐器，给人间的
shēng huó zēng tiān lè qù hé huān lè yì tiān fú xī xún shì dào xī shān
生活增添乐趣和欢乐。一天，伏羲巡视到西山
tóng lín zhǐ jiàn jīn mù shuǐ huǒ tǔ wǔ xīng de jīng líng fēn fēn piāo
桐林，只见金、木、水、火、土五星的精灵，纷纷飘
luò zài wú tóng shù shang dùn shí shù de zhōu wéi shǎn xiàn jīn sè de guāng
落在梧桐树上。顿时，树的周围闪现金色的光
máng piāo dàng zhe měi miào de yīn yuè tiān kōng zhōng yǒng xiàn jí xiáng de
芒，飘荡着美妙的音乐，天空中涌现吉祥的
yún cǎi shàng miàn tuō zhe liǎng zhī měi lì de dà niǎo piān piān jiàng luò zài
云彩，上面托着两只美丽的大鸟，翩翩降落在
nà kē wú tóng shù shang zhè shí qí yú de niǎo er men yě dōu fēn fēn jù
那棵梧桐树上。这时，其余的鸟儿们也都纷纷聚
jí zài zhōu wéi de shù shāo shang cháo zhe nà liǎng zhī měi lì de dà niǎo dà
集在周围的树梢上，朝着那两只美丽的大鸟大
shēng de jiào zhe fú xī kàn dào zhè yì qíng jǐng hòu shí fēn jīng yì tā
声地叫着。伏羲看到这一情景后，十分惊异，他
xiǎng nán dào zhè jiù shì chuán shuō zhōng de fèng huáng ma yòu tīng jiàn
想："难道这就是传说中的凤凰吗？"又听见
nà liǎng zhī dà niǎo jí zú jí zú de jiào qǐ lái le páng biān de bǎi niǎo
那两只大鸟"即足即足"地叫起来了，旁边的百鸟
yě dōu yì qí gēn zhe jiào le qǐ lái fǎng fú zhèng zài zhù fú hé cháo bài
也都一齐跟着叫了起来，仿佛正在祝福和朝拜。

fú xī zhè cái zhī dào nà ge jiào shēng jí jí de shì xióng niǎo shì fèng
伏羲这才知道那个叫声“即即”的是雄鸟，是凤；
nà ge jiào shēng zú zú de shì cí niǎo shì huáng yīn wèi fèng huáng shì
那个叫声“足足”的是雌鸟，是凰。因为凤凰是
bǎi niǎo zhī wáng néng gòu gǎn yìng tiān dì tōng líng shén wù tā yí dìng
“百鸟之王”，能够感应天地，通灵神物，它一定
yào yù dào wú tóng shù cái huì qī xī suǒ yǐ fú xī rèn wéi fèng huáng
要遇到梧桐树才会栖息。所以，伏羲认为，凤凰
jiàng lín de zhè kē dà shù kěn dìng shì shén líng zhī wù fú xī fēi cháng xīn
降临的这棵大树肯定是神灵之物。伏羲非常欣
xǐ duì zhe nà kē wú tóng shù wān yāo jū gōng biǎo dá gǎn xiè tā gōng jìng
喜，对着那棵梧桐树，弯腰鞠躬表达感谢，他恭敬
de shuō dào zhè shì huáng tiān jiàng xià fú zhǐ cì yǔ rén men yǐ fú lè
地说道：“这是皇天降下福祉，赐予人们以福乐
ya rán hòu tā kǎn xià nà kē wú tóng shù
呀。”然后，他砍下那棵梧桐树。

fú xī bǎ wú tóng shù dài huí jiā yǐ hòu jīng guò fǎn fù shì yàn zuì
伏羲把梧桐树带回家以后，经过反复试验，最
hòu zhì chéng le yí jiàn jīng qiǎo jué lún de yuè qì suí hòu tā yòu fǎng zhào
后制成了一件精巧绝伦的乐器。随后他又仿照
bǎi niǎo cháo fèng de qíng jǐng chuàng zào le jià biàn yuè qǔ gòng rén tán
“百鸟朝凤”的情景创造了《驾辩》乐曲，供人弹
chàng jù shuō měi dāng rén jiān qìng hè fēng shōu hé jié rì de shí hou rén
唱。据说每当人间庆贺丰收和节日的时候，人
men chú le yào bàn fēng shèng de yàn xí hái yào tán zòu fú xī chuàng zào de
们除了要办丰盛的宴席，还要弹奏伏羲创造的
yuè qì hēng chàng tā chuàng zuò de yuè qǔ zhè kuài lè xiāo yáo de chǎng
乐器，哼唱他创作的乐曲。这快乐逍遥的场
miàn lìng nà xiē tiān shàng de shén xiān shí fēn xiàn mù
面，令那些天上的神仙十分羡慕。

hòu lái tiān gōng zhōng de wáng mǔ niáng niang zài yáo chí yàn qǐng tiān shén
后来，天宫中的王母娘娘在瑶池宴请天神。

wèi le gěi dà jiā zhù xìng tā tè dì ná lái fú xī chuàng zào de yuè qì dāng
为了给大家助兴，她特地拿来伏羲创造的乐器当

chǎng yǎn zòu tiān shén men jiàn zhè yuè qǔ dòng tīng yuè qì qí tè biàn gěi tā
场演奏。天神们见这乐曲动听，乐器奇特，便给它

qǔ le yí gè míng zi jiào zuò qín yīn wèi yòu shì dì yī cì zài yáo chí
取了一个名字，叫作“琴”。因为又是第一次在瑶池

jiàn dào tiān shén men biàn jiāng fú xī suǒ chuàng de yuè qì chēng wéi yáo qín
见到，天神们便将伏羲所创的乐器称为“瑶琴”。

cóng cǐ rén jiān biàn yǒu le gǔ lǎo de yuè qì qín
从此，人间便有了古老的乐器——琴。

According to Chinese legend, Fuxi was the child of a heaven god for his mother Huaxu stepped into the footprint left by the god, became pregnant and finally gave birth to Fuxi. Therefore, Fuxi was born with superpower with which he set up his kingdom in the East after he grew up. As the emperor, Fuxi taught people skills and constantly came to the earth to take care of them: he brought fire to them, changing their raw-food eating habit; he imparted way of fishing to them by imitating the spider's net weaving way to weave fishing nets. In this way, Fuxi continually brought benefits to human beings.

Later, Fuxi felt the life on the earth was boring and dull, and then he invented a musical instrument to bring joy and fun to the earth. One day, when he was making an inspection tour to the phoenix trees in the West Mountain, he saw the five spirits of Gold, Wood, Water, Fire and Earth all rested on the phoenix trees. Instantly, those trees sparked with golden lights with flowing music. Meanwhile, in the sky, there appeared propitious clouds on which stood two beautiful giant birds. They flew down and landed on the phoenix tree. At that time, all the rest birds gathered to the branches shouting towards the two beautiful giant birds. Upon seeing the scene, Fuxi was shocked and wondered whether the two giant birds were the phoenixes in legend. It was when he heard the two giant birds crying with the sounds of "ji zu, ji zu" and all the rest birds followed to cry as if they were all blessing and worshiping the two giants birds than he realized the giant bird crying with the sound "ji, ji" was the male bird named Feng and the other one crying with the sound "zu, zu" was the female bird named Huang. The phoenix was the king of birds whose heart can feel the response from the heaven and the earth as well as the holy spirits. Only on phoenix trees would it rest. So, Fuxi believed the phoenix tree on which the phoenixes were willing to rest was surely a holy thing. Joyfully, Fuxi bent towards the tree and said sincerely with respect "You are the blessing from the Emperor and will give people happiness and joy". Then he chopped down the phoenix tree.

Fuxi brought the phoenix tree back home. After repeated trying, he finally made a delicate instrument. Later, he created the music "Jia Bian" for people to enjoy themselves by imitating the scene of birds paying homage to the phoenix. According to Chinese legend, whenever it came to the time of harvest or festival, people would have a feast, play the instrument invented by Fuxi and hum the music of "Jia Bian". The merry and happy scene aroused the admiration of those immortals in the heaven.

Later, the Queen of the Heaven played the instruments made by Fuxi for entertainment when she held a Yaochi feast for the gods. Seeing the special instrument, gods named it Qin after enjoying the touching music played with it. As it first appeared in Yaochi, then the instrument was called Yao Qin (peptachord). Since then, on the earth, there was an old instrument named Qin.

故事点评 | Story Comment

这个神话生动展现了上古神器伏羲琴的诞生，这预示着我国琴文化的开端。从此，中华民族拥有了自己独创的乐器——古琴。据说伏羲琴拥有支配万物心灵的神秘力量，凡是听过伏羲琴琴音的人，能够感到心神宁静祥和。

This myth reflects vividly the born of the ancient musical instrument Fuxi Qin, which predicted the beginning of Chinese Qin culture. Since then, Chinese had a unique instrument: Qin. According to Chinese legend, the Fuxi Qin had a mystical power of controlling the hearts of all the creatures. Whoever enjoyed the music played by the Fuxi Qin would felt peaceful in heart.

门神由来

The Origin of Door Gods

zuì zǎo chū xiàn de mén shén shì shén shū yǔ yù lǜ chuán shuō tā men
最早出现的门神是神荼与郁垒。传说他们

jū zhù zài dù shuò shān shān shàng yǒu yì kē néng zhèn shè bǎi guǐ de táo shù
居住在度朔山，山上有一棵能震慑百鬼的桃树，

táo zhī de dōng běi fāng xiàng yǒu yí dào guǐ mén cháng nián yǒu guǐ hún jìn
桃枝的东北方向，有一道鬼门，常年有鬼魂进

chū shén shū yǔ yù lǜ bǎ shǒu guǐ mén fù zé jiān shì nà xiē wēi hài rén
出。神荼与郁垒把守鬼门，负责监视那些危害人

jiān de è guǐ yí dàn fā xiàn tā men de zōng jì biàn yòng lú wěi zuò de
间的恶鬼，一旦发现它们的踪迹，便用芦苇做的

shéng suǒ bǎ guǐ kǔn bǎng qǐ lái rēng dào shān xià wèi lǎo hǔ hòu lái rén
绳索把鬼捆绑起来，扔到山下喂老虎。后来，人

men biàn jiāng shén shū yǔ yù lǜ de huà xiàng kè zài liǎng kuài táo mù shang guà
们便将神荼与郁垒的画像刻在两块桃木上，挂
zài mén liǎng biān yòng lái qū guǐ bì xié
在门两边用来驱鬼避邪。

dào le táng dài chū xiàn le lìng yí wèi mén shén zhōng kuí tā bú dàn
到了唐代，出现了另一位门神钟馗。他不但
zhuō guǐ ér qiě chī guǐ chuán shuō zhōng kuí cái huá chū zhòng céng jīng qù
捉鬼，而且吃鬼。传说钟馗才华出众，曾经去
cān jiā gōng tíng jǔ bàn de wǔ jǔ kǎo shì dàn yīn zhǎng xiàng chǒu lòu méi yǒu
参加宫廷举办的武举考试，但因长相丑陋没有
zhòng jǔ yú shì nǎo xiū chéng nù zhuàng sǐ zài diàn jiē shang táng gāo zǔ
中举，于是恼羞成怒撞死在殿阶上。唐高祖
tīng shuō hòu wèi tā de gāng liè suǒ gǎn dòng tè cì hóng guān páo jiāng zhōng
听说后为他的刚烈所感动，特赐红官袍将钟
kuí ān zàng
馗安葬。

jù shuō táng xuán zōng yǒu yí duàn shí jiān shēng bìng yǒu tiān wǎn
据说，唐玄宗有一段时间生病。有天晚
shang hū rán mèng jiàn yí gè xiǎo guǐ tōu qiè cái wù tā jí máng jiào rén guò
上忽然梦见一个小鬼偷窃财物，他急忙叫人过
lái zhuō ná xiǎo guǐ zhè shí zhǐ jiàn yí wèi xiàng mào kuí wěi de rén zhuō zhù
来捉拿小鬼。这时只见一位相貌魁伟的人捉住
xiǎo guǐ wā le xiǎo guǐ de yǎn jing jīng guò xún wèn cái zhī dào zhè ge zhuō guǐ
小鬼，挖了小鬼的眼睛，经过询问才知道这个捉鬼
de rén shì zhōng kuí dì èr tiān táng xuán zōng xǐng lái hòu bìng jiù hǎo
的人是钟馗。第二天，唐玄宗醒来后，病就好
le yú shì tā qǐng lái huà jiàng jiāng zhōng kuí de xiàng huà xià lái guà zài
了。于是，他请来画匠将钟馗的像画下来挂在
gōng mén shang zuò wéi mén shén
宫门上作为门神。

yuán dài yǐ hòu bèi sì fèng wéi mén shén de hái yǒu táng dài zhù míng
元代以后，被祀奉为门神的还有唐代著名

jiàng lǐng qín qióng yù chí gōng chuán shuō táng tài zōng yǒu duàn shí jiān
将领秦琼、尉迟恭。传说唐太宗有段时间

shēn tǐ bù shū fu wǎn shang jīng cháng zuò è mèng mèng zhōng yǒu guǐ
身体不舒服，晚上经常做噩梦，梦中有鬼

zài dà hǎn dà jiào tài zōng bǎ zhè ge shì qing gào zhī dà chén wǔ jiàng
在大喊大叫。太宗把这个事情告知大臣，武将

qín qióng yù chí gōng tīng shuō hòu qǐng qiú zài yè wǎn péi hù tài zōng
秦琼、尉迟恭听说后，请求在夜晚陪护太宗。

tài zōng zhǔn xǔ hòu qín qióng yù chí gōng fēn bié zhàn lì zài tài zōng
太宗准许后，秦琼、尉迟恭分别站立在太宗

chuáng tà páng biān shǒu hù tài zōng rù shuì nà tiān wǎn shang tài
床榻旁边，守护太宗入睡。那天晚上，太

zōng shuì de shí fēn ān wěn hòu lái tài zōng mìng lìng huà gōng jiāng èr
宗睡得十分安稳。后来，太宗命令画工将二

rén de huà xiàng xuán guà zài gōng mén shang yòng lái qū guǐ cóng nà yǐ
人的画像悬挂在宫门上用来驱鬼。从那以

hòu gōng zhōng píng ān wú shì
后，宫中平安无事。

The gods Shenshu and Yulü were the first two door gods. According to Chinese legend, they lived in the Dushuo Mountain, where there was a peach tree which could frighten ghosts. At the northeast of the peach tree, a door which ghosts often went in and out was guarded by them. They watched those devils that had harmed people, tied them up with a rope made of reed and threw them down the mountain to feed tigers. Later, people posted two pieces of walnut carved with the images of Shenshu and Yulü on both sides of doors to avoid the ghosts and evil.

Till the Tang Dynasty, there appeared another door god: Zhong Kui who could not only catch ghosts but also eat them. Zhong Kui was a talented intellect. He once took the military examination held in the imperial palace but did not pass the examination for his ugly looking. Feeling angry and humiliated, he bumped into the stairs of the palace and died. Emperor Gaozu appreciated his staunchness and buried him with a granted red robe.

It is said that Emperor Xuanzong of Tang was ill for a long time. One night, he yelled to catch the ghost stealing his property in his dream. Then a big and tall man appeared, caught the ghost and dug its eyes. Emperor Xuanzong later learnt the tall man was named Zhong Kui. The next day, Emperor Xuanzong woke up and found himself already cured. He called a painter to draw the portrait of Zhong Kui and hang it up on the doors of the palace as the door god.

After the Yuan Dynasty, famous generals of the Tang Dynasty like Qin Qiong, Yuchi Gong, etc., were also enshrined as door gods. It was said that Emperor Taizong of Tang felt ill one day for he frequently had nightmares, in which there were ghosts yelling. Emperor Taizong told ministers about the nightmares. Qin Qiong and Yuchi Gong, the generals, asked for accompanying the emperor at night. It was permitted. That night was safe. Later, Emperor Taizong ordered painters to draw the portraits of generals

Qin Qiong and Yuchi Gong and hanged them on the doors of the palace to drive off ghosts. Since then, the palace became peaceful and harmonious.

生难字/词注解 | Notes

神荼：传说中能制伏恶鬼的门神。

Shenshu: Door god who can subdue devils and ghosts, according to the legend.

郁垒：传说中能制伏恶鬼的门神。

Yulü: Door god who can subdue devils and ghosts, according to the legend.

避邪：驱除邪恶或恶魔鬼蜮。

Avoid the ghosts and evil: Drive off the evil, devils and ghosts.

钟馗：中国民间传说中能打鬼驱除邪祟的神。

Zhong Kui: The god who can beat ghosts and drive off the evil in Chinese folk legend.

魁伟：魁梧，身体强壮高大。

Big and tall: A strong-built body.

祀：向神供奉动物或植物、食物、酒类、香烛或珍贵物品作为祭祀。

Offer sacrifice: Offer animals, plants, food, wine, candles or valuables as sacrifices to gods.

故事点评 | Story Comment

门神信仰由来已久，最早源于远古时期的自然崇拜，人们认为万物皆有神灵，门也有神灵附会。在民间影响最深的门神是神荼、郁垒、钟馗、秦琼、尉迟恭，至今仍有许多民众供奉他们。每年的农历十二月三十日晚，人们用桃木雕刻门神放置在大门两侧，以表达辟邪除灾、迎祥纳福的美好愿望。

The worship of door gods has a long history. It originated from the nature worship in ancient times when people believed everything had its god for blessing, so did the door. The most popular door gods among the people were Shenshu, Yulü, Zhong Kui, Qin Qiong and Yuchi Gong who were worshiped and trusted by people widely. Every year at the night of December 30th of the lunar calendar, people laid two pieces of walnut carved with the images of door gods on both sides of doors to express their wishes for the avoidance of ghosts, the evil and disaster and the welcoming of auspiciousness and fortune.

蚕神嫘祖

Silkworm Goddess Leizu

yuǎn gǔ shí hou xī líng shì yǒu yí gè xiǎo nǚ ér míng jiào léi zǔ yǒu
远古时候，西陵氏有一个小女儿名叫嫘祖。有
yí cì tā gēn suí mǔ qīn shàng shān cǎi yě guǒ kàn jiàn yì kē shù shang yǒu hěn duō
一次她跟随母亲上山采野果，看见一棵树上有很多
bái sè guǒ zi tā hěn hào qí jiù xún wèn mǔ qīn zhè shì shén me dōng xi mǔ
白色果子。她很好奇，就询问母亲这是什么东西。母
qīn gào su tā nà shì cán zuò de wō jiào jiǎn fēi cháng jiē shi léi zǔ
亲告诉她，那是蚕做的窝，叫“茧”，非常结实。嫘祖
bǎ cán jiǎn dài huí jiā fàng dào guō lǐ xiǎng bǎ jiǎn zhǔ shú tā yòng guō chǎn bù
把蚕茧带回家，放到锅里想把茧煮熟。她用锅铲不
tíng fān jiǎo jīng qí de fā xiàn cóng jiǎn zhōng chōu chū hěn duō xì sī xì sī yuè jiǎo
停翻搅，惊奇地发现从茧中抽出很多细丝，细丝越搅
yuè duō yuè lā yuè cháng léi zǔ hé mǔ qīn kàn dào yòu ruǎn yòu xì de sī xiàn
越多，越拉越长。嫘祖和母亲看到又软又细的丝线，

非常高兴。她们用蚕丝串起树叶，捆扎东西，十分方便耐用。嫘祖还学蜘蛛结网，把抽出的丝铺挂叠放到树枝上。编得稀了织成网，编得密了织成布。从此丝绸出现了。嫘祖把丝绸做成衣服，穿着又舒服又好看。在嫘祖的带领下，整个西陵氏族都学会了采茧抽丝。嫘祖采茧抽丝、编网织布的美名很快传遍了中原大地。

西陵国有一个相邻的国家，他们的国君是轩辕黄帝。他十分爱慕嫘祖的勤劳与贤惠，就迎娶嫘祖，并册封她为正宫娘娘。嫘祖嫁给轩辕黄帝后，仍然像以前那样，经常跋山涉水，走到乡村田野去传授植桑养蚕、抽丝织布的技术，将她栽桑养蚕的事业推广到了全国。

后来，嫘祖逝世，轩辕黄帝痛不欲生，封嫘祖为“祖神”，意思是养蚕缫丝的创始人。

In ancient times, Xiling had a daughter named Leizu. One day, Leizu went to the hills to gather wild fruits with her mother. Seeing many white fruits on the trees, curious and puzzled, Leizu asked her mother and learnt they were cocoons, very tough coverings made by silkworms. Leizu brought cocoons back home, boiled them in the pot and stirred with spatula without stop. Surprisingly, she found a lot of silk coming out of the cocoons. The more stirring, the more silk would come out and the longer the silk would be. Leizu and her mother were very glad for seeing the soft and fine silk. They used those durable silk to string leaves and wrap up items. Getting a hint from spider's web weaving, Leizu laid and hung silk on the branches. The thinly weaved would be made into nets while the thick would be weaved into cloth. Since then, the silk appeared. Leizu used silk to make clothes which were comfortable and glorious. Gradually, the whole Xiling clan all learnt how to gather cocoons and reel off raw silk. The good name of Leizu for she could gather cocoons, reel off raw silk from cocoons and weave nets and cloth spread around the whole central plains.

The Emperor Huang of Xuanyuan in the neighboring country adored Leizu for her diligence and virtuousness. He married Leizu as empress. Although married to Emperor Huang of Xuanyuan, Leizu still went to the fields in the countryside, crossed the hills and rivers, and imparted the skills of planting mulberry trees and raising silkworms.

Later, Leizu passed away. Emperor Huang of Xuanyuan overwhelmed with grief canonized Leizu as Zu God, the founder of sericulture and silk reeling.

生难字/词注解 | Notes

嫘祖：中国远古时期人物，为西陵氏之女，轩辕黄帝的元妃。

Leizu: A woman lived in ancient times, the daughter of Xiling and the empress of Emperor Huang of Xuanyuan.

翻搅：来回不停搅拌。

Stir: Move something around or mix it in a container using something such as a spoon.

故事点评 | Story Comment

嫘祖采茧抽丝、编网织布，为世界丝绸文化做出巨大贡献，深受百姓敬仰，后人为纪念嫘祖的功绩，尊她为“先蚕娘娘”。

Leizu gathered cocoons, reeled off raw silk from cocoons and weaved nets and cloth, making a great contribution to the world silk culture. She is respected by people. To commemorate her achievements, descendents respectfully call her First Silkworm Empress.

茶神陆羽

Tea God Lu Yu

lù yǔ yì shēng fù yǒu chuán qí sè cǎi tā shì táng dài fù zhōu jìng
陆羽一生富有传奇色彩，他是唐代复州竟
líng jīn hú běi tiān mén rén dà zhì shēng yú gōng yuán nián zú yú
陵（今湖北天门）人，大致生于公元733年，卒于
nián tā yuán xiān shì gè bèi yí qì de gū ér zhí dào táng kāi yuán
804年。他原先是个被遗弃的孤儿，直到唐开元
èr shí sān nián nián lù yǔ bèi lóng gài sì zhù chí zhì jī chán shī
二十三年（735年），陆羽被龙盖寺住持智积禅师
shōu liú kāi shǐ zài sì yuàn zhōng xué xí hái xué huì le zhǔ chá děng shì
收留，开始在寺院中学习，还学会了煮茶等事
wù hòu lái tā lí kāi le sì yuàn wèi le shēng cún tā céng jīng yǎn
务。后来，他离开了寺院。为了生存，他曾经演

guò xì duō shì bàn yǎn chǒu jué xiǎn shì chū le yōu mò jī zhì de cái néng
过戏，多是扮演丑角，显示出了幽默机智的才能。

lù yǔ shí sān suì shí dé dào jìng líng tài shǒu lǐ qí wù de shǎng shí
陆羽十三岁时，得到竟陵太守李齐物的赏识。
lǐ qí wù bù jǐn zèng yǔ tā shī shū hái tuī jiàn tā dào dé gāo wàng zhòng de
李齐物不仅赠予他诗书，还推荐他到德高望重的
xué zhě zōu fū zǐ nà lǐ xué xí zhí zhì shí jiǔ suì xué chéng xià shān lù
学者邹夫子那里学习，直至十九岁学成下山。陆
yǔ yǒu hěn gāo de wén xué bǐng fù yǔ wù xìng xìng gé kuàng dá háo fàng sǎ
羽有很高的文学禀赋与悟性，性格旷达豪放、洒
tuō bù jī hé yán zhēn qīng zhāng zhì hé děng yì pī míng shì chéng wéi hǎo
脱不羁，和颜真卿、张志和等一批名士成为好
yǒu lù yǔ hái jīng cháng hé péng you men yì qǐ yóu shān wán shuǐ pǐn píng
友。陆羽还经常和朋友们一起游山玩水，品评
chá shuǐ tán lùn shī wén cháo tíng tīng shuō lù yǔ hěn yǒu xué wèn jiù shòu
茶水、谈论诗文。朝廷听说陆羽很有学问，就授
yǔ tā guān xián ràng tā dào cháo tíng zuò guān dàn shì lù yǔ bú ài zuò
予他官衔，让他到朝廷做官。但是陆羽不爱做
guān tā dōu tuī tuō bú qù
官，他都推托不去。

èr shí yī suì de shí hou lù yǔ kāi shǐ zhuān xīn yán jiū chá de pǐn
二十一岁的时候，陆羽开始专心研究茶的品
zhǒng hé tè xìng tā lí kāi jìng líng yóu lì tiān xià qù xún fǎng quán guó
种和特性。他离开竟陵，游历天下，去寻访全国
gè dì zhù míng de chá wèi le gèng hǎo de yán jiū cǎi chá zhì chá gōng
各地著名的茶。为了更好地研究采茶、制茶工
yì tā cháng qī yǐn jū zài tiáo xī jīn zhè jiāng wú xīng hòu lái tā zài
艺，他长期隐居在苕溪（今浙江吴兴）。后来他在
miào xǐ sì jū zhù le duō nián dà liàng sōu jí zhěng lǐ yán dú yǒu guān
妙喜寺居住了多年，大量搜集、整理、研读有关

chá de zī liào tā jī lěi duō nián jīng yàn lì jìn láo kǔ zhōng yú xiě chū
茶的资料。他积累多年经验，历尽劳苦，终于写出
le zhōng guó dì yī bù yě shì shì jiè dì yī bù yán jiū chá de zhuān
了中国第一部，也是世界第一部研究茶的专
zhù chá jīng quán shū gòng jì qī qiān duō zì náng kuò chá shù de
著——《茶经》。全书共计七千多字，囊括茶树的
chǎn dì xíng tài shēng zhǎng huán jìng yǐ jí cǎi chá zhì chá yǐn chá de
产地、形态、生长环境以及采茶、制茶、饮茶的
gōng jù hé fāng fǎ děng nèi róng
工具和方法等内容。

chá jīng chéng shū hòu duì zhōng guó chá wén huà de fā zhǎn yǐng
《茶经》成书后，对中国茶文化的发展影
xiǎng jí dà yīn cǐ lù yǔ bèi hòu shì zūn chēng wéi chá shèng sì fèng
响极大，因此陆羽被后世尊称为“茶圣”，祀奉
wèi chá shén
为“茶神”。

Lu Yu had a legendary life. He came from Jingling, Fuzhou in the Tang Dynasty (now Tianmen, Hubei Province). He was an abandoned orphan. In the 23th year of the Kaiyuan era in the Tang Dynasty (735 A.D.), Lu Yu was taken in by Zen master Zhiji, the abbot of Longgai Temple. He studied in the temple including boiling tea. Later, he left the temple and acted in plays, always performing as a clown, showing his humor and wit.

At the age of thirteen, he was appreciated by Jingling Prefect

Li Qiwu who not only gave him books as gifts but also recommended him to the respected scholar Teacher Zou for learning till he was nineteen years old for his high literary talents and wisdom. With a bold, unconstrained, free and uninhibited personality, he made good friends with famous people like Yan Zhenqing, Zhang Zhihe, etc., often travelling with them, tasting tea and talking about poems together. Later the imperial court offered him an official post after learning him as an intelligent man. But he declined.

At the age of twenty one, Lu Yu started to devote himself to the study on the varieties of tea and their features. He left Jingling and travelled around the country to search for famous tea. To study on tea plucking and tea making techniques well, Lu Yu lived a long life of reclusion in Tiaoxi (now Wuxing, Zhejiang Province). Later, he lived in Miaoxi Temple, collecting, collating, studying and reading documents about tea. Over years, he finally wrote the first book on the study of tea, *Tea Classic*, which was also the first book in the world on tea studies. This book contains over seven thousand Chinese characters, including the production place, the morphology and the growing environment of tea trees as well as tea plucking, tea drinking and tea production tools and methods.

Tea Classic had a profound influence on Chinese tea culture. Enshrined as Tea God, Lu Yu was also honored as Tea Sage.

生难字/词注解 | Notes

名士：指有名望但不做官的人或是性情旷达、不拘小节之人。

Famous people: A person with a literary reputation; a celebrity with no official posts.

洒脱不羁：不受约束。

Free and uninhibited: Independent and unconstrained.

囊括：包含了一切事物。

Include: Cover everything.

故事点评 | Story Comment

陆羽一生嗜茶，精于茶道，陆羽能成为茶圣，一是因为他的一生与茶结下了深厚缘分；二是他撰写的茶叶专著《茶经》影响深远。这个故事告诉我们，一个人一生需要用全部心力和意志去做好一件事，以神圣的使命感和责任感去完成一件事，只有这样，才能取得成功，赢得尊重。

Lu Yu loved tea in his whole life. He was a master of tea ceremony. There are two reasons for him to become Tea God. The first one is he had developed a link with tea in his whole life. The second reason is he had written the *Tea Classic*, a

profound tea monograph. His story tells us one needs to focus on one thing in his whole life and try the best with the sacred sense of mission and responsibility. Only then can one win respect and gain success.

中国经典神话故事

第二辑

Part 2

大禹治水

Yu Harnessing the Flood

chuán shuō zài yáo dì shí qī huáng hé liú yù jīng cháng fā shēng hóng
传说在尧帝时期，黄河流域经常发生洪

shuǐ wèi le fáng zhǐ hóng shuǐ fàn làn yáo dì xiàng gè gè bù luò zhēng qiú
水。为了防止洪水泛滥，尧帝向各个部落征求

zhì shuǐ néng shǒu lái píng xī shuǐ huàn
治水能手来平息水患。

yǒu rén tuī jiàn gǔn lái fù zé zhè xiàng gōng zuò gǔn jiē shòu rèn wu
有人推荐鲧来负责这项工作。鲧接受任务

hòu cǎi yòng dī bà wéi dǔ de fāng shì zhì shuǐ jiù shì yòng jiǎn dān de
后，采用“堤坝围堵”的方式治水，就是用简单的

dī bà bǎ jū zhù qū de sì zhōu wéi qǐ lái yǐ dǐ dǎng hóng shuǐ dàn shì
堤坝把居住区的四周围起来以抵挡洪水。但是，

zhè yì fāng fǎ yòng le jiǔ nián dōu méi yǒu chéng gōng dǎng zhù hóng shuǐ de fàn
这一方法用了九年都没有成功挡住洪水的泛

làn yīn cǐ tā bèi yáo dì xià lìng fàng zhú yǔ shān
滥。因此，他被尧帝下令放逐羽山。

shùn dì jì chéng wáng wèi yǐ hòu rèn yòng gǔn de ér zi yǔ lái zhì lǐ
舜帝继承王位以后，任用鲧的儿子禹来治理
shuǐ huàn yǔ méi yǒu yīn wèi fù qīn bèi liú fàng ér chǎn shēng yuàn qì tā
水患。禹没有因为父亲被流放而产生怨气，他
gāo xìng de jiē shòu le zhè yí rèn wu tā dài lǐng zhe duì wu fān shān yuè
高兴地接受了这一任务。他带领着队伍，翻山越
lǐng dào quán guó gè dì qù xún fǎng diào chá zhōng yú zhǎo dào le yì zhǒng
岭，到全国各地去寻访、调查，终于找到了一种
kē xué hé lǐ de zhì shuǐ fāng fǎ jiù shì lì yòng shuǐ cóng gāo chù xiàng dī
科学、合理的治水方法，就是利用水从高处向低
chù shùn liú de zì rán qū shì shùn zhe dì xíng bǎ hé chuān shuǐ liú shū tōng
处顺流的自然趋势，顺着地形把河川水流疏通，
bǎ hóng shuǐ yǐn rù yǐ jīng xiāng tōng de hé dào wā dì huò hú pō shǐ dé
把洪水引入已经相通的河道、洼地或湖泊，使得
hóng shuǐ néng gòu shùn lì de liú rù dà hǎi cóng ér píng xī le shuǐ huàn
洪水能够顺利地流入大海，从而平息了水患。

dà yǔ zhì shuǐ yí gòng huā le shí sān nián de shí jiān tā chuàng zào
大禹治水一共花了十三年的时间。他创造
le yì zhǒng xīn de zhì shuǐ fāng fǎ tóng shí hái fā míng le yuán shǐ cè liáng
了一种新的治水方法，同时还发明了原始测量
gōng jù zhǔn shéng hé guī ju hòu rén gǎn niàn tā de gōng jì wèi
工具——准绳和规矩。后人感念他的功绩，为
tā xiū zhù miào yǔ zūn chēng tā wéi shén yǔ
他修筑庙宇，尊称他为“神禹”。

According to Chinese legend, the Yellow River frequently flooded during the reign of Emperor Yao. To avoid the flooding, Emperor Yao asked for water conservancy experts from tribes.

Gun was recommended to be in charge of this work. After he accepted the task, he used the blocking way to harness the river, i. e. using simple dikes built around the living area to keep back the water. But after being used for 9 years, this method failed. So, he was exiled to the Yu Mountain, ordered by Emperor Yao.

After Emperor Shun succeeded to the throne, Yu, the son of Gun, was appointed to tame the flood. Instead of complaining about his father being exiled, Yu gladly accepted this task. He led his team across the mountains, searched for water conservancy methods throughout the country. Finally, they found a scientific and practical water conservancy method, making use of the flow trend of water, i.e. from the high to the low, to dredge river depending on the local topography so as to lead the flood into those connected rivers, depressions, lakes and eventually into the sea to harness the river.

It took 13 years for Yu to harness the river. He invented a new water conservancy method as well as original measure instruments: the criterion and rule. Appreciating his contributions, the descendents built a temple for him and honored him as Yu God.

生难字/词注解 | Notes

泛滥： 大水漫溢。

Flood: The water overflowing.

鲧： 人名。

Gun: The name of an ancient man.

堵： 阻塞。

Block: To stop something from moving or flowing through.

堤坝： 防水、拦水的建筑物和构筑物。

Dike: A long thick wall that is built to stop water flooding onto a low area of land, especially from the sea.

放逐： 流放。

Exile: To force somebody to leave their country, especially for political reasons or as a punishment.

 | Story Comment

大禹是中国历史上第一位成功治理黄河水患的英雄。在民间，有关他的故事广为流传。如：治水在外十三年，三过家门而不入等。尤其是他在抗洪、治水的过程中表现出的不畏惧艰险、吃苦耐劳的伟大精神，令后人敬佩。

Yu was the first hero in history who successfully harnessed the Yellow River flood. In the folk, his stories were widespread, like during the 13 years, he spent all the time in taming the floods though he passed his home

three times, he did not enter it until his task was completed. He is admired and respected by descendents for his great spirit of not being afraid of hardship and his hard-working spirit showed during the process of flood relief and water conservancy.

精卫填海

The Bird Jingwei Filling the Sea

chuán shuō yán dì yǒu yí gè xiǎo nǚ ér míng jiào nǚ wá shì tā zuì
传说炎帝有一个小女儿，名叫女娃，是他最
xǐ ài de nǚ ér yán dì bù jǐn zhǎng guǎn tài yáng hái fù zé guǎn lǐ
喜爱的女儿。炎帝不仅掌管太阳，还负责管理
wǔ gǔ hé yào cái tā shì qing hěn duō měi tiān yí dà zǎo jiù yào qù dōng
五谷和药材。他事情很多，每天一大早就要去东
hǎi zhǐ huī tài yáng shēng qǐ zhí dào tài yáng luò shān cái huí jiā yīn wèi
海，指挥太阳升起，直到太阳落山才回家。因为
yán dì gōng zuò fán máng méi yǒu shí jiān zhào gù nǚ wá suǒ yǐ nǚ wá
炎帝工作繁忙，没有时间照顾女娃。所以，女娃

jīng cháng yí gè rén dú zì chū qù yóu wán tā fēi cháng xiǎng ràng fù qīn dài
经常一个人独自出去游玩，她非常想让父亲带
tā chū qù dào dōng hǎi tài yáng shēng qǐ de dì fang qù kàn yi kàn kě
她出去，到东海太阳升起的地方去看一看。可
shì fù qīn shì qing tài duō le zǒng shì bú dài tā qù
是父亲事情太多了，总是不带她去。

yì tiān nǚ wá yí gè rén jià zhe yì zhī xiǎo chuán xiàng dōng hǎi tài
一天，女娃一个人驾着一只小船向东海太
yáng shēng qǐ de dì fang huá qù lìng rén yì xiǎng bú dào de shì hǎi shang
阳升起的地方划去。令人意想不到的是海上
tū rán guā qǐ kuáng fēng xià qǐ le bào yǔ bǎ xiǎo chuán xiān fān le nǚ
突然刮起狂风，下起了暴雨，把小船掀翻了。女
wá bèi yān sǐ le dàn shì tā bù gān xīn zhè yàng wú gū de sǐ qù
娃被淹死了。但是，她不甘心这样无辜地死去。
tā de jīng hún huà zuò yì zhī zhǎng zhe huā nǎo dai bái zuǐ ké hóng sè zhuǎ
她的精魂化作一只长着花脑袋、白嘴壳、红色爪
zi de shén niǎo fā chū jīng wèi jīng wèi de bēi míng rén men gěi niǎo qǔ
子的神鸟，发出“精卫、精卫”的悲鸣，人们给鸟取
míng jīng wèi
名“精卫”。

jīng wèi tòng hèn wú qíng de dà hǎi duó qù zì jǐ nián qīng de shēng mìng
精卫痛恨无情的大海夺去自己年轻的生命，
tā fā shì yào bǎ dà hǎi tián píng tā yào bào chóu xuě hèn yīn cǐ tā yí
她发誓要把大海填平，她要报仇雪恨。因此，她一
kè bù tíng de cóng tā zhù de shān shàng xián yí lì xiǎo shí zǐ huò shì yí
刻不停地从她住的山上衔一粒小石子，或是一
duàn xiǎo shù zhī zhǎn chì gāo fēi yì zhí fēi dào dōng hǎi tā zài bō tāo
段小树枝，展翅高飞，一直飞到东海。她在波涛
xiōng yǒng de hǎi miàn shang fēi xiáng zhe bēi míng zhe bǎ shí zǐ shù zhī
汹涌的海面上飞翔着、悲鸣着，把石子、树枝

tóu xià qù xiǎng bǎ dà hǎi tián píng kě shì dà hǎi què réng rán bō tāo
投下去，想把大海填平。可是，大海却仍然波涛

xiōng yǒng sì hū cháo xiào tā bú zì liàng lì
汹涌，似乎嘲笑她不自量力。

jīng wèi méi yǒu qì něi tā měi tiān xián shí zǐ shù zhī rēng xià dà hǎi
精卫没有气馁，她每天衔石子、树枝扔下大海。

rì fù yí rì nián fù yì nián wǎng fù fēi xiáng cóng bù tíng xī rén
日复一日，年复一年，往复飞翔，从不停息。人

men tóng qíng jīng wèi qīn pèi jīng wèi bǎ tā jiào zuò shì niǎo zhì
们同情精卫，钦佩精卫，把它叫作“誓鸟”、“志

niǎo bìng zài dōng hǎi biān shang lì le gè shí bēi shàng miàn kè zhe
鸟”，并在东海边上立了个石碑，上面刻着：

jīng wèi shì shuǐ chù jǐ gè zì
“精卫誓水处”几个字。

According to Chinese legend, there lived a little princess named Nüwa, the youngest daughter of Emperor Yan who loved her most. Emperor Yan was busy for work because he was not only in charge of the sun, but also the food and medicine. Every morning, he went to the East Sea to direct the sun to rise and went back home till the sun set. He was so busy that he didn't have time to take care of his daughter nor to take her to the East Sea where the sun rose for fun. So Nüwa often played outside alone.

One day, she went boating on the East Sea to the place where the sun rose. Unexpectedly, the strong wind rose. It became stormy. The boat was overthrown. Nüwa was drowned to death. She was not reconciled to die unnecessarily and her soul turned into a supernatural bird with a colorful head, a white beak and red claws. Since she mourned herself sadly with the sound "Jingwei, Jingwei", people called it "Jingwei".

Jingwei hated the sea enormously for it took her young life away. She decided to fill up the roaring sea for revenge.

From then on, Jingwei flew to and fro between the mountain and the East Sea, carrying a pebble or a twig and dropping it into the sea, mourning sadly. But the roaring sea seemed to laugh at her.

Jingwei did not give up. She continued to carry twigs or pebbles and dropped them into the sea every day. Day after day, she never stopped. Descendents admired her for her indomitable spirit and called her "Bird under Oath" or "Bird with Will". They set a stone carved with the words "The Place Where Jingwei Vowed to Fill the Sea".

生难字/词注解 | Note

精魂：灵魂，精神。

Soul： The spiritual part of a person, believed to exist after death.

故事点评 | Story Comment

这个故事刻画了勇敢、顽强的精卫鸟形象，反映了古代人民渴望征服大自然的强烈愿望和不畏艰苦、百折不回的毅力。

This story describes the image of a brave and indomitable spirited Jingwei bird, which reflects the strong will of the ancient people to conquer the nature. It also shows the ancient people's indomitable spirit of not being afraid of hardships.

愚公移山

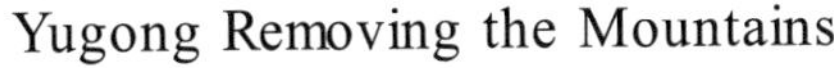

Yugong Removing the Mountains

hěn jiǔ yǐ qián yǒu yí wèi míng jiào yú gōng de lǎo rén tā jiā mén
很久以前，有一位名叫愚公的老人。他家门
kǒu yǒu liǎng zuò dà shān yí zuò shì tài háng shān hái yǒu yí zuò shì wáng wū
口有两座大山，一座是太行山，还有一座是王屋
shān liǎng zuò shān dǎng zài yú gōng jiā de mén kǒu ràng yú gōng měi tiān jìn
山。两座山挡在愚公家的门口，让愚公每天进
chū jiā lǐ dōu yào rào hěn yuǎn de lù
出家里都要绕很远的路。

yì tiān yú gōng gēn jiā rén shāng liang yào dǎ tōng shān lù bǎ dǎng
一天，愚公跟家人商量要打通山路，把挡
zài mén kǒu de liǎng zuò dà shān bān zǒu jiā lǐ de ér sūn men dōu diǎn tóu
在门口的两座大山搬走。家里的儿孙们都点头
zàn chéng kě shì yú gōng de qī zi què bù tóng yì tā shuō bù kě
赞成。可是，愚公的妻子却不同意，她说："不可能的，你年纪这么大了没有多大力气。而且，那些挖出来的泥土石块，你要扔到什么地方去呢？”愚公自信地回答：“那有什么困难的！我们可以把石块丢到海里面去呀！”

第二天，愚公带领儿孙们开始了挖土移山的艰苦劳作。有一个名叫智叟的老人看到愚公移山的行为后，忍不住嘲笑他们说：“愚公呀！你实在太糊涂了。你这么老了，还要去移什么山？别不自量力了，就算让你搬到你死掉的那一天，也不可能把大山移开来的！”

愚公听了他的话，笑笑说：“智叟，你才糊涂呢！我虽然很老了，我还有儿子可以继续去挖呀；儿子还会生孙子，孙子还会再生儿子，我们的子子孙孙可以一直搬下去，只要我们搬掉山的一层，就少一层。总有一天我们会把这两座山搬

zǒu tiān dǐ xia nǎ yǒu bù néng kè fú de kùn nan ne zhì sǒu tīng le hěn
走，天底下哪有不能克服的困难呢？”智叟听了，很
shì cán kuì zhǐ hǎo zǒu kāi le
是惭愧，只好走开了。

hòu lái shān shén hé hǎi shén zhī dào yú gōng yào yí shān de shì qing
后来，山神和海神知道愚公要移山的事情，
dān xīn yú gōng yì jiā rén yǒng bù tíng zhǐ de bān xià qù huì bǎ shān bān
担心愚公一家人永不停止地搬下去，会把山搬
guāng bǎ hǎi tián mǎn tā men jiù pǎo qù gào su tiān dì tiān dì zhī dào
光，把海填满。他们就跑去告诉天帝。天帝知道
zhè jiàn shì hòu fēi cháng gǎn dòng tā shuō zhè ge yú gōng zhēn shì yǒu héng
这件事后非常感动，他说：“这个愚公真是有恒
xīn ya wǒ lái bāng bang tā ba tiān dì jiù pài le liǎng gè shén xiān qù
心呀！我来帮帮他吧！”天帝就派了两个神仙去
bǎ wáng wū shān yǔ tài háng shān bēi zǒu fàng dào bié de dì fang qù liǎng
把王屋山与太行山背走，放到别的地方去，两
zuò shān zài yě bú huì dǎng zài yú gōng jiā mén kǒu le
座山再也不会挡在愚公家门口了。

Long long ago there lived an old man named Yugong. In front of his house, two mountains were located. One was the Taihang Mountain, and the other was the Wangwu Mountain. These two mountains were just in front of his house, making it inconvenient for the family to get around.

One day, Yugong called his family together to discuss how

to move the two mountains and open a way. All the grandchildren agreed, but his wife was against him, saying "It's impossible for an old man like you who is lack of strength to remove the mountains. Besides where can you throw such a large amount of earth and stones?" Yugong and his children all laughed and answered "It's not difficult. We can drop those into the sea."

The next day, Yugong led his grandchildren to break rocks and dig earth. Seeing they were working hard, an old man named Zhisou mocked at Yugong, saying, "How stupid you are! You are so old to remove the high mountains, even if it comes to the day when you die."

Yugong smiled, answering back, "You are not smart enough! I am old. But I have my son. My son will have his son. My grandson will have his son. So generations after generations, there's no end. Once we remove one layer of the mountain, one layer's height would be reduced. There will be a day when we have moved the two mountains. Anything can be done, no matter how difficult it is." Ashamed and humiliated, Zhisou left.

After knowing the story of Yugong, both the Mountain God and the Sea God feared that Yugong with his family would remove the mountains completely. So they told the story to the Emperor of Heaven who was greatly moved by the perseverant spirit of Yugong. He then ordered two gods to take the two high mountains away to other places. Then the two high mountains would never stand in the doorway of Yugong.

生难字/词注解 | Notes

愚公：古人名。

Yugong: The name of an ancient man.

智叟：古人名。

Zhisou: The name of an ancient man.

 | Story Comment

这个故事告诉我们，在生活中需要有愚公精神和志向，无论遇到什么困难，都要勇敢地面对，用坚强乐观和吃苦耐劳的精神去努力奋斗，终有一天，梦想会实现。

This story tells us we need to have the spirit of Yugong in our life: no matter what kind of difficulty we have encountered, we should face it bravely with a strong will and optimism as well as the spirit of hard working to strive for success. One day, our dream will come true.

后羿射日

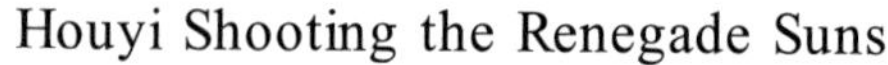

Houyi Shooting the Renegade Suns

chuán shuō gǔ shí hou tiān dì yǒu shí gè tài yáng ér zi tā men xǐ
传说古时候，天帝有十个太阳儿子，他们喜
huān zài liáo kuò de dōng hǎi biān yóu xì wán shuǎ wán lèi le jiù dào fú sāng
欢在辽阔的东海边游戏玩耍，玩累了就到扶桑
shén shù shang xiū xi tā men zhōng yǒu jiǔ gè zài zhǎng de jiào ǎi de shù
神树上休息。他们中有九个在长得较矮的树
zhī shang qī xī lìng yí gè zé zài shù shāo shang qī xī dāng lí míng lái
枝上栖息，另一个则在树梢上栖息。当黎明来
lín de shí hou qī xī zài shù shāo de tài yáng biàn zuò zhe liǎng lún chē chuān
临的时候，栖息在树梢的太阳便坐着两轮车，穿
yuè tiān kōng bǎ guāng hé rè sǎ xiàng zhěng gè rén jiān shí gè tài yáng lún
越天空，把光和热洒向整个人间。十个太阳轮

liú zhí bān měi tiān yí huàn hěn yǒu zhì xù rén men rì chū ér zuò rì
流值班，每天一换，很有秩序。人们日出而作，日
luò ér xī shēng huó guò de hěn ān níng
落而息，生活过得很安宁。

kě shì shí jiān jiǔ le zhè shí gè tài yáng jué de yí gè yí gè de
可是，时间久了，这十个太阳觉得一个一个地
lún liú zhí bān hěn wú liáo tā men xiǎng yào yì qǐ zhōu yóu tiān kōng yú
轮流值班很无聊，他们想要一起周游天空。于
shì lí míng shí fēn shí gè tài yáng yì qǐ pá shàng shuāng lún chē tà
是，黎明时分，十个太阳一起爬上双轮车，踏
shàng le chuān yuè tiān kōng de zhēng chéng zhè yí xià dà dì wàn wù jiù
上了穿越天空的征程。这一下，大地万物就
shòu bu liǎo le shí gè tài yáng xiàng shí gè dà huǒ qiú tā men yì qǐ fàng
受不了了，十个太阳像十个大火球，他们一起放
chū de rè liàng kǎo jiāo le dà dì hé liú yě gān kū le suǒ yǒu de shù
出的热量烤焦了大地，河流也干枯了，所有的树
mù zhuāng jia hé fáng zi dōu bèi shāo chéng le huī jìn sēn lín yě zháo huǒ
木、庄稼和房子都被烧成了灰烬，森林也着火
le rén men rè de kū tiān hǎn dì
了，人们热得哭天喊地。

zhè shí yǒu gè nián qīng yīng jùn de yīng xióng jiào hòu yì tā shì gè
这时，有个年轻英俊的英雄叫后羿，他是个
shén jiàn shǒu jiàn fǎ chāo qún bǎi fā bǎi zhòng tā bèi tiān dì zhào huàn
神箭手，箭法超群，百发百中。他被天帝召唤
qù lǐng shòu le qū gǎn tài yáng de shǐ mìng hòu yì fān shān yuè lǐng lái
去，领受了驱赶太阳的使命。后羿翻山越岭，来
dào le dōng hǎi biān shang dēng shàng le yí zuò miàn lín máng máng dà hǎi de
到了东海边上，登上了一座面临茫茫大海的
dà shān tā lā kāi tiān dì shǎng cì de wàn jīn lì wān gōng dā shàng qiān
大山。他拉开天帝赏赐的万斤力弯弓，搭上千

jīn zhòng de lì jiàn miáo zhǔn tiān shàng huǒ là là de tài yáng sōu de
斤重的利箭，瞄准天上火辣辣的太阳，“嗖”的
yì shēng yí gè tài yáng bèi shè luò le hòu yì yòu lā gōng dā jiàn
一声，一个太阳被射落了。后羿又拉弓搭箭，
wēng de yì shēng liǎng gè tài yáng tóng shí bèi shè luò le zhè xià
“嗡”的一声，两个太阳同时被射落了。这下，
tiān shàng hái yǒu qī gè tài yáng hòu yì gǎn dào zhè xiē tài yáng réng hěn zhì
天上还有七个太阳，后羿感到这些太阳仍很炙
rè yòu hěn hěn de shè chū le dì sān zhī jiàn zhè yí jiàn shè dé hěn yǒu
热，又狠狠地射出了第三枝箭。这一箭射得很有
lì yí xià zi shè luò le sì gè tài yáng qí tā de tài yáng xià de quán
力，一下子射落了四个太阳。其他的太阳吓得全
shēn dǎ chàn dào chù luàn zhuàn
身打颤，到处乱转。

jiù zhè yàng hòu yì yòu lián shè liǎng jiàn jiàn wú xū fā liǎng gè tài
就这样，后羿又连射两箭，箭无虚发，两个太
yáng diào luò xià lái zhòng le jiàn de jiǔ gè tài yáng yí gè jiē yí gè de sǐ
阳掉落下来。中了箭的九个太阳一个接一个地死
qù tā men de yǔ máo fēn fēn luò zài dì shang tā men de guāng hé rè yì
去。他们的羽毛纷纷落在地上，他们的光和热一
diǎn yì diǎn de xiāo shī le rén men dùn shí gǎn dào qīng liáng shuǎng kuai zuì hòu
点一点地消失了，人们顿时感到清凉爽快。最后
shèng xià yí gè tài yáng tā shí fēn hài pà jiù ān zhào hòu yì de fēn fù
剩下一个太阳，他十分害怕，就按照后羿的吩咐，
měi tiān cóng dōng bian shēng qǐ bàng wǎn zài cóng xī bian luò xià lǚ xíng zì jǐ
每天从东边升起，傍晚再从西边落下，履行自己
de zhí zé jì xù bǎ guāng hé rè pǔ zhào dào rén jiān
的职责，继续把光和热普照到人间。

According to Chinese legend, the Emperor of Heaven had ten sun sons. They liked playing by the vast East Sea, and if feeling tired, they would rest on the Fusang tree. Nine of them rested on the lower branches of the tree while the other rested on a higher place. When dawn came, the one which rested on the higher place would drive a two-wheeled cart, going across the sky, to shine brightly to the earth. The ten suns did the task in turn. Every day, people went out to work at daybreak and went back home when the sun set. People led a peaceful life.

But as time went on, they felt boring to appear in the sky alone every day. They wanted to be in the sky all together. When dawn came, the ten suns climbed to the cart and went across the sky, shining like ten big fire balls. Instantly, the land was burned; the rivers dried up; all the woods, crops and houses were burned into ashes; people cried out for not being able to bear the heat.

The Emperor of Heaven was extremely angry and ordered a handsome and skillful archer, Houyi, who had superb archery skills and never missed a shot, to punish them. Crossing mountains after mountains, Houyi came to the East Sea. He climbed on the top of a mountain facing the sea, pulled the bow which was honored by the Emperor of Heaven and set an arrow of more than one thousand *jin* (= five hundred kilograms) on it. He aimed at a hot sun and shot it down accurately. Then he pulled another bow, this time two suns were shot down. There were still seven suns in the sky. Houyi still felt hot, then he shot out another arrow with great strength which hit four suns down at one time. The rest suns were scared and ran around.

Houyi went on shooting out another two arrows and shot down two suns. At last, nine suns were shot down and died gradually. Their light and heat disappeared with their feathers scattering around on the ground. Instantly, people felt cool again. The only one remained was scared and did his duty, rising from the east and setting in the west, to give light and heat to the earth as required by Houyi.

故事点评 | Story Comment

在民间被封为"箭神"的后羿神勇非凡：他上射太阳、下杀猛兽，一心为民除害。后羿射日的英勇壮举，千百年来为人们所称道，反映了我国古代劳动人民渴望战胜自然、改造自然的美好愿望。

Among the folk, Houyi, honored as Bow Master, was especially brave. He shot the suns and killed the fierce monsters to eradicate harm for common people. His heroic feat of shooting down nine suns has been talked and appreciated by people for thousands of years. The story reflects ancient laborers' good wishes to conquer and transform the nature.

杜康酿酒

Dukang Making Wine

dù kāng shì huáng dì de yì yuán dà chén fù zé guǎn lǐ liáng shi
杜康是黄帝的一员大臣，负责管理粮食
shēng chǎn tā bǎ liáng shi chǔ cún zài shān dòng lǐ hòu lái yīn wèi liáng shi
生产。他把粮食储存在山洞里，后来因为粮食
shòu dào yǔ shuǐ jìn pào fā shēng méi biàn dù kāng bèi huáng dì chè le zhí
受到雨水浸泡发生霉变，杜康被黄帝撤了职，
biǎn wéi yì míng bǎo guǎn liáng shi de xiǎo zú
贬为一名保管粮食的小卒。

yǒu yí cì dù kāng zài sēn lín lǐ fā xiàn jǐ kē kū sǐ de dà shù
有一次，杜康在森林里发现几棵枯死的大树，

树身里边都空了。于是，他将大树掏空，修理，将粮食全部装进树洞加以保存。谁知过了两年多，树洞中的粮食经过长期风吹日晒雨淋，慢慢开始发酵了。一天，杜康上山查看粮食情况，发现有两只山羊走到大树跟前，用舌头使劲舔着树洞，过了一会儿，山羊就东倒西歪，没走多远，就躺倒在地。

杜康走过去一看，原来装粮食的树洞，已裂开缝，不断地往外渗水。山羊就是舔食这水才睡倒的。杜康俯身去闻这种渗出的液体，闻到特别的芳香。他尝了一口，觉得有些甜中带涩，但气味特别浓香。于是，他又不由自主地多喝了几口，不一会儿时间，他觉得天旋地转，身子倒下去，呼呼地睡着了。醒来后他觉得神清气爽，很有劲儿。

dù kāng bǎ zhè ge shén qí de jīng lì xiàng huáng dì bào gào huáng dì pǐn
杜康把这个神奇的经历向黄帝报告。黄帝品
cháng zhè zhǒng fāng xiāng nóng yù de shuǐ hòu dà wéi zàn shǎng jiù hé dà chén men
尝这种芳香浓郁的水后，大为赞赏，就和大臣们
shāng yì bìng qǐng cāng jié chuàng zào yí gè zì lái mìng míng tā nà jiù shì
商议，并请仓颉创造一个字来命名它，那就是
jiǔ hòu rén wèi le jì niàn dù kāng zūn chēng tā wéi niàng jiǔ shǐ zǔ
“酒”。后人为了纪念杜康，尊称他为“酿酒始祖”。

Dukang, a minister of Emperor Huang, who was in charge of food production, was demoted to a private to protect food because the food stored in caves by him was soaked in rain and became mildewed.

Once, Dukang found several withered trees with empty trunks. He emptied those trees and stored food there. Over two years, the food in the tree holes began to ferment after being exposed to all the forces of wind and different kinds of weather. One day, Dukang went up to the mountain to check food. He found two goats come up to one tree and lick the tree holes hard. For a while, the two goats staggered like drunken men. They had not gone far away before they laid on the ground.

Dukang went over and found the tree holes where the food stored have cracked, from which water came out and the two goats fell in sleep for drinking the water. Coming near to smell the fragrance of the water, Dukang had a taste and found a strong sweet, astringent flavor and aroma of the water. He could not help to take several more sips. After a while, he felt the sky and the earth were spinning around and fell down to sleep. After waking up, he felt cool and full of strength.

Dukang reported this unusual experience to Emperor Huang who later tasted the fragrant water and appreciated it. Then Emperor Huang discussed with his ministers and invited Cangjie to create a Chinese character "Jiu" to name it as wine. Descendents honored Dukang as "The Father of Wine-Making" to commemorate him.

生难字/词注解 | Notes

霉变: 衣服、食品等受了潮热长霉菌。

Mildew: A thin whitish coating consists of minute fungal hyphae, growing on plants or damp organic material such as paper or leather.

卒: 士兵。

Private: A soldier of the lowest rank in the army.

发酵: 有机物由于某些真菌或酶而分解。

Ferment: A chemical change because of the action of yeast or bacteria, often changing sugar to alcohol.

舔: 用舌头接触东西。

Lick: To eat or drink something by licking it.

故事点评 | Story Comment

这个故事告诉我们在日常生活中要善于发现，勇于创新，勇于承担责任，积极探寻自然奥秘与事物本源。只有这样，才能获得成功。

This story tells us we should be good at discovering in our daily life. We need to be brave to be innovative and be responsible to explore the miracles of nature and the origin of matters, by which we can gain success.

杜鹃啼血

The Cuckoo Crying Blood

gǔ shí hou shǔ guó yǒu yí gè huáng dì míng jiào dù yǔ hào wàng
古时候，蜀国有一个皇帝名叫杜宇，号望
dì tā xīn xì tiān xià ài mín rú zǐ
帝，他心系天下，爱民如子。

yǒu yì nián shǔ guó zāo yù hóng zāi rén men shēng huó hěn bēi cǎn
有一年，蜀国遭遇洪灾，人们生活很悲惨。
wèi zhěng jiù bǎi xìng yú shuǐ huǒ zhī zhōng tā xià zhào cè fēng shén tōng guǎng
为拯救百姓于水火之中，他下诏册封神通广
dà de biē líng wéi chéng xiàng ràng tā qù xùn fú hóng shuǐ hòu lái hóng shuǐ
大的鳖灵为丞相，让他去驯服洪水。后来洪水
bèi biē líng zhì fú wàng dì wèi le huí bào biē líng jiù jiāng wáng wèi ràng
被鳖灵制服。望帝为了回报鳖灵，就将王位让
gěi le tā zì jǐ zé yǐn jū xī shān
给了他，自己则隐居西山。

biē líng dāng shàng le guó wáng hào cóng dì tā dài lǐng shǔ guó rén
鳖灵当上了国王，号丛帝。他带领蜀国人
mín xīng xiū shuǐ lì kāi kěn tián dì zuò le xǔ duō lì guó lì mín de hǎo
民兴修水利，开垦田地，做了许多利国利民的好

shì kě shì cóng dì hòu lái biàn de jiāo ào zì mǎn dú duàn zhuān
事。可是，丛帝后来变得骄傲自满，独断专

quán wàng dì zhī dào cóng dì de xíng wéi hòu fēi cháng zháo jí xī
权。望帝知道丛帝的行为后，非常着急，希

wàng néng gòu quàn shuō cóng dì yì xīn xiàng shàn rán ér yào jiàn dào cóng
望能够劝说丛帝一心向善。然而，要见到丛

dì bìng bù róng yì shān gāo lù yuǎn cóng dì yòu jǐn bì chéng mén
帝并不容易。山高路远，丛帝又紧闭城门，

wàng dì gēn běn jiù wú fǎ jìn rù gōng zhōng wèi le jìn jiàn cóng dì
望帝根本就无法进入宫中。为了觐见丛帝，

wàng dì zhǐ hǎo huà zuò yì zhī dù juān niǎo fēi rù gōng zhōng gāo shēng jiào
望帝只好化作一只杜鹃鸟飞入宫中，高声叫

zhe mín guì ya mín guì ya cóng dì tīng le zhī hòu shòu dào gǎn
着："民贵呀！民贵呀！"丛帝听了之后受到感

dòng hěn nèi jiù cóng nà yǐ hòu cóng dì gǎi zhèng yǐ qián de kuáng
动，很内疚。从那以后，丛帝改正以前的狂

wàng zì fù gèng jiā qín miǎn yú zhèng shì wèi bǎi xìng fú lì zhuó xiǎng
妄自负，更加勤勉于政事，为百姓福利着想，

chéng wéi yí dài míng jūn
成为一代明君。

kě shì wàng dì yǐ jīng huà chéng le dù juān niǎo wú fǎ zài biàn huí
可是，望帝已经化成了杜鹃鸟，无法再变回

yuán xíng le yóu yú qiān guà zhe tiān xià bǎi xìng tā měi cì zài fēi xiáng shí
原形了。由于牵挂着天下百姓，他每次在飞翔时

jiù fā chū mín guì ya mín guì ya de jiào shēng zhí dào shēng yīn sī
就发出"民贵呀！民贵呀！"的叫声。直到声音嘶

yǎ hóu lóng chū xuè xiān xuè dī zài shān gǔ lǐ jìn rǎn le yí cù cù shèng
哑，喉咙出血，鲜血滴在山谷里，浸染了一簇簇盛

kāi de huā huā sè rú xuè xiān yàn duó mù hòu rén wèi le jì niàn wàng
开的花，花色如血，鲜艳夺目。后人为了纪念望

帝，将此花取名叫杜鹃花，将杜鹃鸟取名叫“杜宇鸟”，也叫“子归鸟”。

In ancient times, in the Shu Kingdom, there was an emperor named Duyu, with the assumed name Emperor Wang. He loved and cared the common people.

One year, the whole country suffered flooding, which made people live in misery. To save the common people, Emperor Wang sent out an imperial decree to appoint omnipotent Bieling as prime minister to conquer the flood. Finally the flood was tamed by Bieling. To reward Bieling for what he had done, Emperor Wang gave the throne to him and led a seclude life in the West Mountain.

Bieling became the emperor with the assumed name Emperor Cong. He led people to do many good deeds like water conservancy projects, cultivation of fields for farming and so on. But later Emperor Cong became conceited, arrogant and autocratic. Upon knowing it, Emperor Wang became anxious to persuade Emperor Cong to change. However, the distance was long and the mountain was high. As Emperor Cong had closed the city gate, Emperor Wang had to change into a cuckoo (Dujuan bird) to fly into the palace, crying loudly “people being the most important, people being the most important”. Emperor Cong felt guilty and moved. Since then, he was more diligent in government matters

and became a wise emperor, thinking about people's benefits. Because Emperor Wang had changed into a cuckoo, he could not turn back into his original shape. As he always thought about people, every time he was flying, he would cry till his voice became hoarse and his throat bleeding. The blood dropped into valleys, dying the blooming flowers brightly with the blood color. To commemorate Emperor Wang, descendents named the flowers as azalea (Dujuan flower) and cuckoo as Duyu bird or Zigui bird.

生难字/词注解 | Note

蜀：先秦时候的古蜀国。

The Shu Kingdom: An ancient state in what is now Sichuan Province of China.

故事点评 | Story Comment

望帝身为一国之君，始终心系百姓。他适时地规劝丛帝，最后献出生命，他身上体现出来的以人为本、大公无私的精神，令后人敬仰。

As the head of state, Emperor Wang always thought about people. For persuading Emperor Cong, he finally lost his life. He is honored and respected by descendents for his people-oriented and selfless spirit.

观音送画

Goddess Guanyin Sending Pictures

guān yīn pú sà yòu chēng guān shì yīn pú sà shì sì dà pú sà zhī yī tā xiàng mào duān zhuāng cí xiáng xīn dì shàn liáng shǒu lǐ jīng cháng ná zhe yí gè chā le yáng liǔ de jìng píng zhān le jìng píng zhōng de shuǐ jiù jù yǒu qǐ sǐ huí shēng de shén qí fǎ lì jù shuō zài rén men yù dào zāi nàn de shí hou zhǐ yào niàn qí míng hào tā jiù kě yǐ tīng jiàn shì shàng kǔ

观音菩萨，又称观世音菩萨，是四大菩萨之一。她相貌端庄慈祥，心地善良，手里经常拿着一个插了杨柳的净瓶，沾了净瓶中的水就具有起死回生的神奇法力。据说在人们遇到灾难的时候，只要念其名号，她就可以听见世上苦

nàn de shēng yīn suǒ yǐ bèi chēng wéi guān shì yīn
难的声音，所以被称为“观世音”。

yǒu yì nián háng zhōu bǎi xìng shōu cheng bù hǎo jiā jiā hù hù dōu méi
有一年，杭州百姓收成不好，家家户户都没
yǒu duō shǎo liáng shi jī huāng shǐ dà jiā fēi cháng kǒng jù bú xìng de
有多少粮食。饥荒使大家非常恐惧。不幸的
shì chéng lǐ yòu bào fā wēn yì bǎi xìng pín bìng jiāo jiā hěn duō rén bú shì
是城里又暴发瘟疫，百姓贫病交加。很多人不是
bèi è sǐ jiù shì gǎn rǎn shàng wēn yì bēi cǎn de sǐ qù rén men zài zhè
被饿死，就是感染上瘟疫，悲惨地死去。人们在这
chǎng zāi nàn zhōng qí qiú shàng tiān de bǎo yòu qí dǎo de shēng yīn xiǎng chè
场灾难中，祈求上天的保佑，祈祷的声音响彻
yún tiān
云天。

yì tiān chéng biān de hú pō zhōng tíng kào le yì sōu dà chuán
一天，城边的湖泊中，停靠了一艘大船，
chuán tóu zuò le yí wèi duān zhuāng měi lì de nǚ zǐ rén men dōu hěn chà
船头坐了一位端庄美丽的女子。人们都很诧
yì kě shì zhè ge nǚ zǐ què hěn cóng róng tā duì dà jiā shuō xiàn zài shì
异，可是这个女子却很从容，她对大家说，现在是
duō zāi duō nàn de nián fèn dà jiā yào qí xīn xié lì dù guò nán guān nà
多灾多难的年份，大家要齐心协力渡过难关。那
xiē qióng rén yóu qí xū yào bāng zhù rú guǒ yǒu rén chū qián mǎi tā tā jiù
些穷人尤其需要帮助，如果有人出钱买她，她就
zhù zài tā de jiā lǐ wèi tā dài lái fú zhǐ rán hòu tā huì bǎ qián yòng
住在他的家里，为他带来福祉。然后，她会把钱用
lái jiù jì pín kǔ de rén men
来救济贫苦的人们。

àn shang de rén tīng shuō hòu shí fēn gǎn dòng dōu zhēng qiǎng zhe yào
岸上的人听说后，十分感动，都争抢着要

mǎi tā dàn shì zhè me duō rén gāi qù shéi jiā lǐ ne yú shì dà jiā
买她。但是，这么多人该去谁家里呢。于是，大家
jiù cǎi yòng tóu qián de fāng fǎ shéi bǎ qián tóu dào tā shēn shang jiù yíng
就采用投钱的方法，谁把钱投到她身上，就迎
jiē tā huí qù yí huìr shí jiān hěn duō qián dōu fēn fēn tóu xià lái duī
接她回去。一会儿时间，很多钱都纷纷投下来，堆
mǎn le chuán tóu què méi yǒu yì méi luò zài tā shēn shang dà jiā shí fēn
满了船头，却没有一枚落在她身上。大家十分
shī wàng zhī hǎo fàng qì nǚ zǐ wēi wēi de xiào zhe shuāng shǒu hé zhǎng
失望，只好放弃。女子微微地笑着，双手合掌
xiàng àn shang de rén biǎo dá zhēn chéng de gǎn xiè suí hòu bǎ qián dōu shī shě
向岸上的人表达真诚的感谢，随后把钱都施舍
gěi le qióng rén
给了穷人。

zhè ge shì qing hōng dòng le zhěng gè háng zhōu chéng fù rén men wèi
这个事情轰动了整个杭州城。富人们为
tā xiá yì de xíng wéi gǎn dòng fēn fēn kāng kǎi de juān wù juān qián gěi nà xiē
她侠义的行为感动，纷纷慷慨地捐物捐钱给那些
pín kǔ de rén yú shì bìng rén ná dào le qián jiù qù kàn bìng qióng rén
贫苦的人。于是，病人拿到了钱就去看病，穷人
dé dào qián kě yǐ wéi chí shēng huó jī è de rén yǒu le qián kě yǐ mǎi dào
得到钱可以维持生活，饥饿的人有了钱可以买到
shí wù měi gè rén dōu yǒu suǒ dé gǎn dào shí fēn mǎn zú hé kuài lè
食物。每个人都有所得，感到十分满足和快乐。
zhěng gè chéng lǐ dōu xiǎn de qì fēn róng qià hé mù zhè shí dà jiā fā
整个城里都显得气氛融洽、和睦。这时，大家发
xiàn yuán xiān nà ge shàn liáng shī shě de nǚ zǐ zuò de chuán shang shǎn xiàn
现，原先那个善良施舍的女子坐的船上闪现
jīn guāng nà ge nǚ zǐ huà wéi yí wèi fǎ xiàng zhuāng yán de pú sà tā
金光，那个女子化为一位法相庄严的菩萨，她

hé zhǎng wēi xiào cí xiáng de kàn zhe dà jiā shuō wǒ jiù shì guān shì yīn
合掌微笑，慈祥地看着大家说：“我就是观世音

pú sà wǒ lái zhè lǐ shì wèi le qǐ fā hé huàn xǐng dà jiā de shàn xīn
菩萨，我来这里，是为了启发和唤醒大家的善心。

tóng qíng lián mǐn shì zuì gāo guì de pǐn zhì bāng zhù tā rén shì zuì shén shèng
同情、怜悯是最高贵的品质，帮助他人是最神圣

de zé rèn jīn tiān dà jiā de biǎo xiàn hěn hǎo zhí dé zàn měi dà jiā
的责任。今天，大家的表现很好，值得赞美，大家

dōu jiāng dé dào xìng fú zài chǎng de rén tīng shuō hòu fēi cháng gāo xìng
都将得到幸福。”在场的人听说后，非常高兴，

dōu hé qǐ shǒu zhǎng niàn sòng guān shì yīn pú sà guān shì yīn pú sà
都合起手掌，念诵“观世音菩萨”。观世音菩萨

bǎ huà xiàng sòng gěi tā men bìng qiě tā yìng cheng zì jǐ de nuò yán zhēn
把画像送给他们。并且她应承自己的诺言，真

de zhù zài měi yí wèi chū qián wéi shàn de rén jiā lǐ
的住在每一位出钱为善的人家里。

cóng cǐ zhè ge gù shi bú duàn de liú chuán yuè lái yuè duō de rén
从此，这个故事不断地流传，越来越多的人

xìn fèng guān shì yīn pú sà
信奉观世音菩萨。

Goddess Guanyin, also called the Goddess Guanshiyin is one of the four Bodhisattvas. She is respectable and dignified with a warm and kind heart. She always brings a holy bottle with willows in it with her. The water in the holy water has a magic power that

can bring the dying back to life. According to Chinese legend, she could learn people's suffering once people called her name when facing danger or disaster. So she is called the Goddess Guanshiyin.

One year, for bad harvest, people living in Hangzhou were all horrified by famine. Unfortunately, a plague broke out in the city. Many people died of starvation or plague in misery. People prayed towards the heaven whose sounds roared in the heaven.

One day, on the lake of the city floated a big ship in which sat a beautiful lady. People felt puzzled but that lady said calmly to the mass that this year was full of disasters, people should work together to overcome the difficulties. The poor needed help particularly. If the rich were willing to buy her, she would come home with him and bring luck to him. With that amount of money she would save the poor.

People standing on the bank were moved and all scrambled and strove to be the first to buy her. But there would be only one who could buy her back home. Then all agreed to throw money to the lady. The one who threw the money on the lady could bring her back home. In a while, a large amount of money was thrown to the lady and piled up in the ship's bow, but none of the money was thrown on the lady. Those rich people were disappointed and had to give up. Smiling, the lady clapped her hands and showed her sincerity to the people. Later, she gave that money to the poor.

The whole thing surprised the city. The rich were all moved by her kindness and all donated stuff and money to the poor generously. The sick people went to see doctors with the donated money while the poor could buy food with the money. Everyone felt contented and happy. The whole city seemed peaceful and harmonious. Then, people found the ship where the lady sat was glowing with golden light. The lady changed back into a dignified Bodhisattva image who smiled, clapped her hands and said to the mass: "I am Goddess Guanyin. I come here to invoke your kindness and generosity. Sympathy and compassion are noble characters. Helping others is the holiest responsibility. Today, you all behaved well and are worthy of being praised and blessed. All of you will be happy." People were happy and clapped their hands, praying and blessing Goddess Guanyin. Goddess Guanyin gave them a picture and fulfilled her promise to live in those people's houses who had donated their money to the poor.

Since then, the story spread widely which enhanced people's belief in Goddess Guanyin.

故事点评 | Story Comment

观世音菩萨大慈大悲,行善积德,能救苦救难,消除灾祸,在民间备受人们的敬仰和爱戴。现代很多人都佩戴观音吊坠,寓意保佑平安,吉祥如意。

The Bodhisattva Goddess Guanyin is kind and generous and always helps people out from disasters and sorrow. She is admired and respected by people. In modern life, many people wear Guanyin pendants with the wish for luck and blessing.

尧舜禅让

Yao and Shun Abdicating and Handing Over the Crown

chuán shuō huáng dì zhī hòu zài huáng hé liú yù de bù luò chū xiàn guò
传说黄帝之后，在黄河流域的部落出现过

yáo shùn yǔ sān gè zhù míng de huáng dì yáo shì dì kù de ér zi
尧、舜、禹三个著名的皇帝。尧是帝喾的儿子、

huáng dì de wǔ shì sūn yáo xīn huái tiān xià duì lǎo bǎi xìng shī xíng rén
黄帝的五世孙。尧心怀天下，对老百姓施行仁

zhèng zài tā de zhì lǐ xià rén mín ān jū lè yè rán ér yáo zài wèi
政。在他的治理下，人民安居乐业。然而，尧在位

qī shí nián hòu nián jì dà le tā jué dìng xuǎn bá yí gè xián néng de rén
七十年后，年纪大了，他决定选拔一个贤能的人

lái jiē tì zì jǐ de wáng wèi yú shì yáo dì zhào jí gè bù zú shǒu lǐng
来接替自己的王位。于是，尧帝召集各部族首领

yì qǐ shāng liang yáo de ér zi dān zhū cū sú wú lǐ jīng cháng nào shì
一起商量。尧的儿子丹朱粗俗无礼，经常闹事，
yǒu rén tuī jiàn dān zhū jì wèi yáo bù tóng yì
有人推荐丹朱继位，尧不同意。

hòu lái yáo yòu zhào kāi huì yì zài cì tǎo lùn jì chéng rén de wèn tí
后来尧又召开会议，再次讨论继承人的问题。
dà jiā tuī jǔ shùn zuò wéi wáng wèi jì chéng rén shuō tā shì gè dé cái jiān
大家推举舜作为王位继承人，说他是个德才兼
bèi hěn yǒu cái gàn de rén yáo hěn gāo xìng bǎ zì jǐ de liǎng gè nǚ ér
备，很有才干的人。尧很高兴，把自己的两个女儿
é huáng nǚ yīng jià gěi shùn bìng zài jīng guò sān nián de kǎo yàn hòu cái
娥皇、女英嫁给舜，并在经过三年的考验后，才
jiāng dì wèi shàn ràng gěi shùn zhè shí hou shùn gāng mǎn sān shí suì
将帝位禅让给舜。这时候，舜刚满三十岁。

shùn jì chéng wáng wèi hòu qīn zì gēng tián dǎ yú zhì táo shēn
舜继承王位后，亲自耕田、打鱼、制陶，深
shòu bǎi xìng ài dài shùn nián lǎo shí yě fǎng zhào yáo de zuò fǎ ràng dà
受百姓爱戴。舜年老时，也仿照尧的做法让大
chén tuī jiàn xián dé zhī rén zuò wáng wèi jì chéng rén yǔ shì dà jiā gōng rèn
臣推荐贤德之人做王位继承人。禹是大家公认
de xián míng zhī rén yú shì zài shùn jià bēng hòu yǔ zuò le bù luò lián
的贤明之人。于是，在舜驾崩后，禹做了部落联
méng de shǒu lǐng hòu lái zhè zhǒng yóu dà jiā mín zhǔ tuī xuǎn jǔ jiàn
盟的首领。后来，这种由大家民主推选、举荐
wáng wèi jì chéng rén de zuò fǎ bèi chēng wéi shàn ràng
王位继承人的做法，被称为“禅让”。

After Emperor Huang, there appeared other three famous emperors like Yao, Shun and Yu in the tribes along the Yellow River. Yao was the son of Emperor Ku, the fifth generation descended from the Emperor Huang. He cared greatly about his country and practiced benevolent governance to people, which helped people to lead a happy and peaceful life. However, after seventy years being an emperor, Yao was old and decided to choose a good and able man for the throne. Then, Yao called on the heads of all tribes to discuss. One man recommended Danzhu, the son of Yao, for the throne. Yao disagreed for his son being rude, outrageous and always making troubles.

Later, Yao held a meeting again to discuss the matter. Shun was recommended for being able and capable with political integrity. Yao was delighted and let his two daughters, Ehuang and Nüying, marry to Shun. After three years' tests, Yao abdicated and handed over the crown to Shun who just turned thirty at that time.

After Shun succeeded to the throne, he plowed, fished and made pottery himself, and was loved and respected by people. When Shun was old, he followed the practice of Yao and asked ministers to recommend able person with political integrity as the successor to the throne. Yu was recommended as the good and wise man. Then after Shun demised, Yu became the head of the tribal league. Later, the practice of choosing successor of the throne by democratic election was called abdication.

生难字/词注解 | Notes

禅让：中国古代历史上统治权转移的一种方式，皇帝把帝位让给他人。

Abdication: The action of transferring sovereignty in ancient times in Chinese history. The emperor gives up the position of being king or throne to others.

喾：传说中的上古帝王名。

Emperor Ku: The name of an emperor in ancient times.

驾崩：中国古代称皇帝或皇太后的死亡为"驾崩"。

Demise: The death of king or empress dowager in ancient China.

故事点评 | Story Comment

这个故事表现了尧、舜为了国家利益，顾全大局、公正廉明的高尚情操。他们开创的"禅让"方式反映出了原始公社的政治民主制度，体现了"以人为本，任人唯贤"的思想，有利于民族团结，促进生产力发展。

This story shows Yao and Shun's impartiality, integrity and their noble sentiments for taking the public interests into account. The abdication way they created reflected the political democratic system of primitive commune, which showed the thought of "People-oriented, appointing people by their merit." It was beneficial for national unity and the development of productivity.

夸父逐日

Kuafu Racing with the Sun

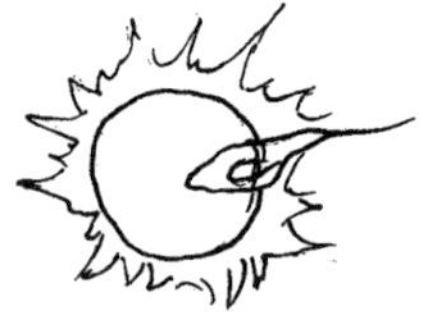

yuǎn gǔ shí hou zài běi fāng de shēn shān lǎo lín lǐ jū zhù zhe yì
远古时候，在北方的深山老林里，居住着一

qún lì dà wú qióng de jù rén tā men de shǒu lǐng míng zi jiào zuò kuā
群力大无穷的巨人。他们的首领，名字叫作“夸

fù yīn cǐ zhè qún rén jiù jiào kuā fù zú yǒu yì nián tiān qì fēi
父”，因此这群人就叫“夸父族”。有一年，天气非

cháng yán rè huǒ là là de tài yáng zhí shè zài dà dì shang tǔ dì gān
常炎热，火辣辣的太阳直射在大地上，土地干

liè cǎo mù kū wěi yǒu hěn duō rén jīn bú zhù liè rì pù shài ér sǐ qù
裂，草木枯萎，有很多人禁不住裂日曝晒而死去。

kuā fù hěn bēi tòng tā gào su zú rén yào qù zhuī gǎn tài yáng
夸父很悲痛，他告诉族人要去追赶太阳。

kuā fù gào bié zú rén mài kāi dà bù yí lù zhuī gǎn tài yáng jīng guò
夸父告别族人，迈开大步一路追赶太阳。经过

jiǔ tiān jiǔ yè kuā fù zhōng yú zài tài yáng luò shān de dì fang zhuī shàng le
九天九夜，夸父终于在太阳落山的地方追上了

tā nà shí tā de tóu shang xiá guāng wàn zhàng yáng guāng sǎ luò zài
它。那时，他的头上，霞光万丈，阳光洒落在

tā shēn shang kuā fù wú bǐ huān xīn de zhāng kāi shuāng bì xiǎng bǎ tài
他身上。夸父无比欢欣地张开双臂，想把太

yáng bào zhù kě shì tài yáng tài yán rè le kuā fù gǎn dào yòu lèi yòu kě
阳抱住。可是太阳太炎热了，夸父感到又累又渴。

tā pǎo dào huáng hé biān yì kǒu qì bǎ huáng hé shuǐ hē gān le kě hái shì bù
他跑到黄河边，一口气把黄河水喝干了，可还是不

jiě kě tā yòu pǎo dào wèi hé biān bǎ wèi hé shuǐ yě hē guāng le réng bù
解渴。他又跑到渭河边，把渭河水也喝光了，仍不

jiě kě kuā fù yòu jì xù xiàng běi pǎo qù nà lǐ yǒu zòng héng qiān lǐ de
解渴。夸父又继续向北跑去，那里有纵横千里的

dà zé dà zé lǐ de shuǐ zú gòu kuā fù jiě kě dàn shì dà zé tài yuǎn
大泽，大泽里的水足够夸父解渴。但是，大泽太远，

kuā fù hái méi yǒu pǎo dào dà zé jiù zài bàn lù shang bèi kě sǐ le
夸父还没有跑到大泽，就在半路上被渴死了。

kuā fù lín sǐ de shí hou xīn lǐ chōng mǎn yí hàn tā hái qiān guà
夸父临死的时候，心里充满遗憾。他还牵挂

zhe zì jǐ de zú rén jiù jiāng zì jǐ shǒu zhōng de mù zhàng rēng chū qù
着自己的族人，就将自己手中的木杖扔出去，

mù zhàng luò xià de dì fang dùn shí shēng chū dà piàn mào shèng de táo lín
木杖落下的地方，顿时生出大片茂盛的桃林。

chuán shuō zhè piàn táo lín zhōng nián mào shèng shù zhī shang guà mǎn xiān táo
传说这片桃林终年茂盛，树枝上挂满鲜桃，

gòng lù rén jiě kě
供路人解渴。

In ancient times, in the north thick-forested mountains, there lived a group of giants with great strength. The head was Kuafu, so this group was named Kuafu tribe. One year, it got particular hot as the burning sun scorched the earth which caused the ground to dry up and plants wither to die. Many people could not stand the heat and died. Kuafu was sorrowful and told his clansmen that he would go to chase the sun.

Parted with his clansmen, he strode and begun his journey. After nine days and nights, he finally caught up with the sun at the place where the sun set. At that time, the glowing and burning hot sun shone over him. Kuafu was extremely excited and pleased that he opened his arms to hold the sun. But the sun was too hot that Kuafu felt tired and thirsty. He ran to the Yellow River and in one drink he drained the water. But he still felt thirsty. Then he went to the Wei River and drained the water. Not having quenched his thirst, Kuafu ran to the north where there was the Ze River with a thousand *li* in both length and width. The water in the Ze River was enough for him. But the Ze River was so far away that Kuafu died of thirst on his way back.

While he was dying, he was full of regrets but still cared about his clansmen. Then he dropped the cane in his hand to the ground which turned into a large peach grove, being lush all year round. The branches hung with fresh peaches, helping passers-by to quench their thirst.

生难字/词注解 | Note

炎热：形容温度极高。

Hot: With a high temperature.

故事点评 | Story Comment

这个故事表现了夸父勇往直前的英雄气概和为后人造福的伟大精神，反映了古代先民积极探索，渴望征服大自然的强烈愿望和顽强意志。

This story shows Kuafu's heroic spirit of marching forward courageously and his great spirit of making benefits for the descendents. It reflects that ancient people were actively exploring the nature and their strong will to conquer the nature.

刑天舞干戚

Xingtian Brandishing Ganqi

chuán shuō tiān dì yǒu duàn shí jiān chén jìn yú shēng huó xiǎng lè bú
传说天帝有段时间沉浸于生活享乐，不
gù bǎi xìng sǐ huó yīng xióng xíng tiān fēi cháng fèn nù tā jué de tiān shén
顾百姓死活。英雄刑天非常愤怒，他觉得天神
yīng gāi yì xīn wèi mín qín miǎn zhèng shì rán ér tiān dì gēn běn bù tīng
应该一心为民，勤勉政事。然而，天帝根本不听
quàn gào xíng tiān wèi le zhěng jiù rén mín yú shuǐ huǒ zhī zhōng jué dìng yào
劝告。刑天为了拯救人民于水火之中，决定要
duì kàng tiān dì tā zuǒ shǒu wò zhe dùn pái yòu shǒu ná zhe dà fǔ yí lù
对抗天帝，他左手握着盾牌，右手拿着大斧，一路
shā guò lái tiān dì kàn jiàn xíng tiān nù qì chōng chōng de shā lái zhǐ děi
杀过来。天帝看见刑天怒气冲冲地杀来，只得
yíng zhàn liǎng rén jiàn lái fǔ pī nǐ lái wǒ wǎng cóng tiān gōng nèi shā
迎战。两人剑来斧劈，你来我往，从天宫内杀

dào tiān gōng wài cóng tiān shàng shā dào rén jiān zhí shā dào cháng yáng shān de
到天宫外，从天上杀到人间，直杀到常羊山的
páng biān
旁边。

tiān dì bì jìng jiǔ jīng shā chǎng qiě yǒu jiǔ tiān xuán nǚ chuán shòu de
天帝毕竟久经沙场，且有九天玄女传授的
bīng fǎ zài dǎ dòu zhōng tā kàn dào le xíng tiān de yí gè pò zhàn yí jiàn
兵法，在打斗中他看到了刑天的一个破绽，一剑
xiàng xíng tiān de jǐng bó kǎn qù shùn shí xíng tiān de tóu lú gǔn luò xià lái
向刑天的颈脖砍去，瞬时刑天的头颅滚落下来，
luò zài cháng yáng shān jiǎo xià xíng tiān dǎ de zhèng zài xìng tou shang zhǐ
落在常羊山脚下。刑天打得正在兴头上，只
fā jué bó zi shang liáng liáng de tā yòng shǒu yì mō fā xiàn méi le tóu
发觉脖子上凉凉的。他用手一摸发现没了头
lú dùn shí jīng huāng qǐ lái jí máng sì chù xún zhǎo tiān dì dān xīn xíng
颅，顿时惊慌起来，急忙四处寻找。天帝担心刑
tiān zhēn de mō dào tóu lú tā yòng lì jiāng cháng yáng shān pī wéi liǎng bàn
天真的摸到头颅，他用力将常羊山劈为两半，
xíng tiān de tóu lú gū lū lū de luò rù shān zhōng liǎng shān yòu hé ér wéi
刑天的头颅骨碌碌地落入山中，两山又合而为
yī bǎ tóu lú shēn shēn de mái zàng qǐ lái
一，把头颅深深地埋葬起来。

tīng dào zhè yì yàng de xiǎng shēng xíng tiān zhī dào zì jǐ de tóu lú
听到这异样的响声，刑天知道自己的头颅
bèi mái zàng zài shān jiǎo zhī xià le tā jiāng yǒng yuǎn shēn shǒu yì chù dàn
被埋葬在山脚之下了，他将永远身首异处。但
tā bù gān xīn jiù zhè yàng bài zài tiān dì shǒu xià shī qù tóu de xíng tiān
他不甘心就这样败在天帝手下。失去头的刑天
bǎ shēn qū dàng zuò tóu lú bǎ liǎng rǔ dàng zuò yǎn jing dù qí dàng zuò
把身躯当作头颅，把两乳当作眼睛，肚脐当作

kǒu jì xù fèn zhàn tiān dì kàn jiàn wú tóu xíng tiān fèn nù de huī wǔ dùn
口，继续奋战。天帝看见无头刑天愤怒地挥舞盾

fǔ jīn bú zhù yí zhèn zhàn lì bù yóu hài pà qǐ lái gǎn jǐn táo huí tiān
斧，禁不住一阵战栗，不由害怕起来，赶紧逃回天

tíng qù le
庭去了。

According to Chinese legend, there was a time when the Emperor of Heaven was addicted to life enjoyment, not caring about people's life. Hero Xingtian felt furious because he believed gods should be diligent in political affairs for the people. However, the Emperor of Heaven did not accept Xingtian's advice and still persisted in his old way. Xingtian decided to fight with the Emperor of Heaven. With a shield in the left hand and a huge axe in the right hand, Xingtian fought his way to the heaven. Upon seeing it, the Emperor of Heaven had no other choice but to accept the fight. They fought fiercely from the inside of the heavenly palace to the outside, from the heaven to the earth.

After all, the Emperor of Heaven was experienced in fighting; besides he had military strategy and tactics taught by the Goddess of the Empyrean. During the fight, the Emperor of Heaven found out one weakness of Xingtian and used his sword to cut Xingtian's neck. Instantly, the head of Xingtian fell down from the neck to the foot of the Changyang Mountain. Devoted to the fight,

Xingtian felt cool at his neck. Only when his hand touched his neck than he knew what had happened. Being in panic, he hurried to search for his head. Fearing Xingtian would find the head, the Emperor of Heaven halved the Changyang Mountain with his sword. Then the head of Xingtian fell in before the two halves became one again. The head was buried under the mountain deeply.

Hearing the strange sound, Xingtian knew his head had been buried and would forever be apart from the body. He was not reconciled to his defeat. Without his head, Xingtian used the body as head, two breasts as eyes, and navel as mouth and went on fighting. Seeing Xingtian without head still waving the shield and axe furiously, the Emperor of Heaven was scared and fled back to the heavenly palace in terror.

生难字/词注解 | Notes

干戚： 干，盾牌；戚，大斧。

Ganqi: Gan, shield; Qi, axe.

肚脐： 肚子中间脐带脱落的地方。

Navel: The small hollow part or lump in the middle of the stomach where the umbilical cord was cut at birth.

Story Comment

刑天为了天下万民，公然与最高统治者天帝做斗争，虽然战败，但刑天不畏强权、绝不服输的精神，为后人称颂。

For the common people, Xingtian fought with the monarch, the Emperor of Heaven, openly. Although defeated, Xingtian is honored and appreciated by descendents for his spirit of not fearing power and never surrendering.

鲤鱼跳龙门

Carp Jumping over the Dragon Gate

hěn zǎo hěn zǎo yǐ qián lóng mén hái wèi záo kāi yī shuǐ liú dào zhè lǐ
很早很早以前，龙门还未凿开，伊水流到这里
bèi lóng mén shān dǎng zhù le jiù zài shān nán jī jù le yí gè dà hú jū
被龙门山挡住了，就在山南积聚了一个大湖。居
zhù zài huáng hé lǐ de lǐ yú tīng shuō lóng mén fēng jǐng hěn měi dōu hěn xiǎng
住在黄河里的鲤鱼听说龙门风景很美，都很想
guò qù yóu wán yì fān
过去游玩一番。

yì tiān zhè xiē lǐ yú chéng qún jié duì yí lù hào hào dàng dàng de
一天，这些鲤鱼成群结队，一路浩浩荡荡地
cóng huáng hé chū fā tōng guò luò hé yòu shùn yī hé lái dào lóng mén shuǐ jiàn
从黄河出发，通过洛河，又顺伊河来到龙门水溅

kǒu de dì fang kě shì lóng mén shān shàng méi yǒu shuǐ lù kě yǐ shàng
口的地方。可是，龙门山上没有水路可以上

qù tā men zhǐ hǎo jù zài lóng mén de shān jiǎo xià yì qǐ shāng liang bàn fǎ
去，它们只好聚在龙门的山脚下一起商量办法。

tū rán yì tiáo dà hóng lǐ yú duì dà jiā shuō wǒ yǒu gè zhǔ yi zán
突然，一条大红鲤鱼对大家说："我有个主意，咱

men tiào guò zhè lóng mén shān zěn yàng qí tā lǐ yú dōu yáo yáo tóu shuō
们跳过这龙门山怎样？"其他鲤鱼都摇摇头，说

nà me gāo zěn me tiào a tiào bù hǎo huì shuāi sǐ de dà jiā dōu
"那么高，怎么跳啊？""跳不好会摔死的！"大家都

zài nà lǐ yóu yù bù jué ná bú dìng zhǔ yi hái shì nà tiáo dà hóng lǐ
在那里犹豫不决，拿不定主意。还是那条大红鲤

yú shuō wǒ xiān tiào shì yi shì huà gāng shuō wán zhǐ jiàn tā cóng
鱼说："我先跳，试一试。"话刚说完，只见它从

yuǎn chù jiù shǐ chū quán shēn lì qi yòng jìn zòng shēn yí yuè yí xià zi tiào
远处就使出全身力气，用劲纵身一跃，一下子跳

dào bàn tiān yún lǐ dài dòng zhe kōng zhōng de yún hé yǔ wǎng qián zǒu yì
到半天云里，带动着空中的云和雨往前走。一

tuán tiān huǒ cóng shēn hòu zhuī lái shāo diào le tā de wěi ba tā rěn zhe
团天火从身后追来，烧掉了它的尾巴。它忍着

téng tòng jì xù cháo qián fēi yuè zhōng yú yuè guò lóng mén shān luò dào shān
疼痛，继续朝前飞跃，终于越过龙门山，落到山

nán de hú shuǐ zhōng yì zhǎ yǎn jiù biàn chéng le yì tiáo jù lóng
南的湖水中，一眨眼就变成了一条巨龙。

qí tā de lǐ yú men kàn jiàn zhè yàng de qíng xíng yí gè gè bèi xià de
其他的鲤鱼们看见这样的情形，一个个被吓得

suō zài yí kuàir bù gǎn zài qù mào zhè ge xiǎn le zhè shí hū jiàn tiān
缩在一块儿，不敢再去冒这个险了。这时，忽见天

shàng jiàng xià yì tiáo jù lóng shuō bú yào pà wǒ jiù shì nǐ men de huǒ bàn
上降下一条巨龙说："不要怕，我就是你们的伙伴

dà hóng lǐ yú yīn wèi wǒ tiào guò le lóng mén jiù biàn chéng le lóng nǐ men
大红鲤鱼,因为我跳过了龙门,就变成了龙,你们

yě yào yǒng gǎn de tiào ya lǐ yú men tīng le zhè xiē huà shòu dào gǔ wǔ
也要勇敢地跳呀!”鲤鱼们听了这些话,受到鼓舞,

kāi shǐ yí gè gè āi zhe tiào lóng mén shān kě shì chú le gè bié de tiào guò
开始一个个挨着跳龙门山。可是除了个别的跳过

qù huà wéi lóng yǐ wài dà duō shù dōu guò bú qù fán shì tiào bú guò qù
去化为龙以外,大多数都过不去。凡是跳不过去,

cóng kōng zhōng shuāi xià lái de é tóu shang jiù luò yí gè hēi bā zhí dào jīn
从空中摔下来的,额头上就落一个黑疤。直到今

tiān zhè ge hēi bā hái zhǎng zài huáng hé lǐ yú de é tóu shang ne
天,这个黑疤还长在黄河鲤鱼的额头上呢。

hòu lái táng cháo dà shī rén lǐ bái zhuān mén wèi zhè jiàn shì xiě le yì
后来,唐朝大诗人李白专门为这件事写了一

shǒu shī huáng hé sān chǐ lǐ běn zài mèng jīn jū diǎn é bù chéng
首诗:“黄河三尺鲤,本在孟津居。点额不成

lóng guī lái bàn fán yú
龙,归来伴凡鱼。”

Long long ago, there was no Dragon Gate. When the Yi River flowed to the Dragon Gate Mountain, it would turn back, which formed a big lake in the south of the mountain. As the carps living in the Yellow River heard that the scenery in the Dragon Gate Mountain was beautiful, they all wanted to travel there.

One day, from the Yellow River, these carps in groups swam

along the Yi River, passing the Luo River, to the Dragon Gate Mountain where the water was blocked back to the lake as there was no road to the Dragon Gate Mountain directly. They all rested at its foot. Suddenly, a big red carp claimed that they could jump over the Dragon Gate Mountain. All the rest shook their heads against him for fearing they wound die if trying out for jumping over the high mountain. When all the rest were hesitating and had no idea, that big red carp jumped into the half sky and the clouds with all its strength, not long before it claimed to have a try, which drove the clouds and rains moving forward. A crowd of fire from the heaven chased it up and burned down its tail. Under great pains, it still went on jumping and finally jumped across the Dragon Gate Mountain and fell down into the lake in the south of the mountain. In a second, it became a giant dragon.

The rest carps felt scared and huddled together. They did not dare to take a risk. Then in a sudden, from the heaven there flew down a giant dragon who said: "Don't be afraid, I am your mate, the big red carp. I changed into a dragon because of my jumping over the Dragon Gate. You should be brave to jump as well." Inspired, the rest carps jumped over the Dragon Gate one by one. Except for a few jumped over the Dragon Gate, most of them could not pass the gate and would fall down and bump into the ground with a black scar on the forehead. Till now, this black scar still could be seen on the forehead of the carps the Yellow River.

Later, the great poet of the Tang Dynasty, Li Bai, wrote a poem for the carps: "Carp in the Yellow River, lived in Mengjin. It failed to jump over, only left with scar, and come back to live with the common ones."

故事点评 | Story Comment

鲤鱼跳过龙门，就会变化成龙，这一神话故事在我国民间具有独特的文化意义。它比喻升学、升官等光宗耀祖的喜事。现在也用来形容人们在逆境中敢于接受挑战，奋发向上，有所作为。

The carp jumping over the Dragon Gate could change into a dragon. This myth has a unique cultural significance among the folk. It has a metaphorical meaning of the happy events bringing glory to one's ancestors like entering a higher level school, getting a promotion, etc. Now it is used to describe people with the braveness to take challenge, strive hard and make achievements.

二月二龙抬头

February 2, the "Dragon Rise"

chuán shuō wǔ zé tiān dāng shàng nǚ huáng dì rě nǎo le yù huáng dà
传说武则天当上女皇帝，惹恼了玉皇大
dì yú shì tā chuán mìng tài bái jīn xīng gào su sì hǎi lóng wáng sān nián
帝。于是，他传命太白金星告诉四海龙王，三年
nèi bù dé xiàng rén jiān jiàng yǔ yǐ shì chéng jiè yǐ zhì dà dì gān hé
内不得向人间降雨，以示惩戒，以致大地干涸，
zhuāng jia hàn sǐ xǔ duō dì fang lián hē shuǐ dōu fēi cháng kùn nan bǎi xìng
庄稼旱死，许多地方连喝水都非常困难，百姓
shēng huó kǔ bù kān yán
生活苦不堪言。

zhǎng guǎn tiān hé de yù lóng hěn tóng qíng rén men de zāo yù biàn wéi
掌管天河的玉龙很同情人们的遭遇，便违
kàng yù huáng dà dì zhǐ yì wèi rén jiān jiàng le yì chǎng dà yǔ yù
抗玉皇大帝旨意，为人间降了一场大雨。玉
huáng dà dì zhī dào hòu jiù bǎ yù lóng biǎn dào rén jiān yā zài yí zuò dà
皇大帝知道后，就把玉龙贬到人间，压在一座大

shān jiǎo xià shòu kǔ shān qián lì le yí kuài shí bēi shàng miàn kè zhe yì
山脚下受苦，山前立了一块石碑，上面刻着一

shǒu shī yù lóng xíng yǔ fàn tiān guī yīng shòu rén jiān qiān qiū zuì ruò
首诗："玉龙行雨犯天规，应受人间千秋罪，若

xiǎng chóng shàng líng xiāo diàn chú fēi jīn dòu kāi huā shí
想重上凌霄殿，除非金豆开花时。"

rén men jīng guò zhè lǐ kàn dào shí bēi shang de zhè xiē zì cái zhī dào
人们经过这里，看到石碑上的这些字，才知道

yù lóng yīn wéi fàn tiān mìng wèi le zhěng jiù bǎi xìng jiàng xià dà yǔ què bèi
玉龙因违犯天命，为了拯救百姓降下大雨，却被

yā zài zhè lǐ shòu kǔ wèi le jiù chū yù lóng shǐ tā chóng shàng tiān tíng
压在这里受苦。为了救出玉龙，使他重上天庭

qù zhǎng guǎn tiān hé rén men jué xīn zhǎo dào kāi huā de jīn dòu zhǎo a
去掌管天河，人们决心找到开花的金豆。找啊、

zhǎo a zhí dào dì èr nián de nóng lì èr yuè chū yī zài jiē dào shang
找啊，直到第二年的农历二月初一，在街道上，

yǒu yí gè lǎo nǎi nai bēi zhe yí dài zi yù mǐ lì zǒu zhe zǒu zhe bù xiǎo xīn
有一个老奶奶背着一袋子玉米粒，走着走着不小心

jīn huáng de yù mǐ lì sǎ le yí dì rén men kàn dào le fēi cháng gāo
金黄的玉米粒撒了一地。人们看到了，非常高

xìng yīn wèi zhè yù mǐ lì duō xiàng jīn dòu ya rú guǒ fàng zài guō lǐ
兴。因为这玉米粒多像金豆呀！如果放在锅里

chǎo bú jiù bào chū jīn huā le ma
炒，不就爆出金花了吗？

yú shì yì chuán shí shí chuán bǎi dà jiā quán dōu zhī dào le tā
于是，一传十，十传百，大家全都知道了。他

men yì qǐ yuē hǎo dào èr yuè chū èr zhè yì tiān yì qí xíng dòng dà jiā dōu
们一起约好到二月初二这一天，一齐行动，大家都

bào yù mǐ huā bìng zài yuàn zi lǐ shè àn fén xiāng gòng shàng kāi le huā
爆玉米花，并在院子里设案焚香，供上开了花

de jīn dòu dāng yù huáng dà dì kàn jiàn rén jiān jiā jiā hù hù yuàn zi
的“金豆”。当玉皇大帝看见人间家家户户院子

lǐ dōu jīn dòu huā kāi fàng zhǐ hǎo chuán zhào lóng wáng chóng xīn huí dào
里都金豆花开放，只好传诏龙王重新回到

tiān tíng
天庭。

cóng cǐ měi nián nóng lì èr yuè chū èr zhè yì tiān rén men jiù bào yù
从此，每年农历二月初二这一天，人们就爆玉

mǐ huā qìng zhù lóng wáng chóng fǎn tiān tíng
米花，庆祝龙王重返天庭。

According to Chinese legend, the fact that Wu Zetian became the empress irritated the Emperor of Heaven who later gave Taibai Jinxing an imperial decree which was told to the four Sea Dragon Kings that they were not allowed to give rain to the earth in three years as punishment for the earth, which caused the earth dried up, the crops withered and dying and people living in misery.

The Sea Dragon King (Jade Dragon) in charge of the Heavenly River felt sympathy for the people. He made a heavy rain down to the earth against the imperial decree of the Emperor of Heaven. After learning it, the Emperor of Heaven exiled the Sea Dragon King to earth and suppressed him under the foot of a mountain in front of which stood a stone tablet carved with a poem "Jade dragon making rain against heavenly rule, should be punished by the earthly sin; if wanted to return back to the heavenly palace, unless golden beans bloom."

It was when people passed by the stone than they got to know why the Sea Dragon King was suppressed under the foot of the mountain. To give rain to people, he was against the imperial decree and thus punished to be there for suffering. To save the Sea Dragon King, people searched for the bloomed golden beans. Till next year, on lunar February 1, an old woman carried a bag of maize seeds but they were poured out on the ground by accident. People felt glad when seeing those seeds look like the golden beans. If those seeds were fried, they all would bloom which signified "golden beans bloom".

The news travelled fast. All the people knew the way to rescue the Sea Dragon King. Then every family fried maize seeds, set a table with burning incense and placed bloomed maize seeds as golden beans in the yard on the lunar February 2. After seeing all the families on the earth had bloomed golden beans in the yard, the Emperor of Heaven had to give the imperial decree to call back the Sea Dragon King to the heavenly palace.

Since then, there formed a custom that each year when it came to the lunar February 2, people would fry the maize seeds and celebrate the returning of the Sea Dragon King to heaven.

生难字/词注解 | Note

凌霄殿：传说中天君玉皇大帝的宫殿。

Heavenly palace: The palace where the Emperor of Heaven lives according to Chinese legend.

故事点评 | Story Comment

每年农历二月二，又称“春耕节”“农事节”“青龙节”，传说是龙抬头的日子，是汉族民间传统节日。人们在这一天举行隆重的庆祝仪式，以表达敬龙祈雨、五谷丰登的美好愿望。

The lunar February 2 of each year is also called “Royal Ploughing Day”, “Farming Festival”, and “Blue Dragon Festival”. According to Chinese legend, it was the day when the dragon raised the head. This day was a traditional Han people's folk festival when people would hold a celebration to show their respect for the dragon and their wish for rainfall and good harvests.

中国经典神话故事

第三辑

Part 3

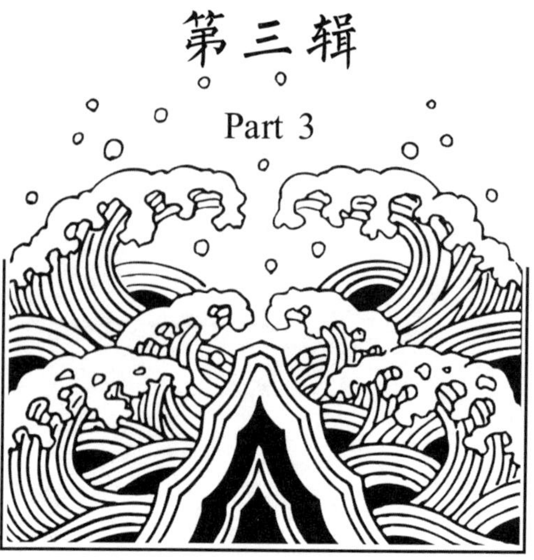

月下老人

The Old Man under the Moon

chuán shuō zài táng dài yǒu yí gè jiào wéi gù de rén yí cì lù guò
传说在唐代有一个叫韦固的人，一次路过

sòng chéng jīn hé nán shāng qiū wǎn shang jiè sù zài yì jiā míng jiào nán
宋城（今河南商丘），晚上借宿在一家名叫“南

diàn de lǚ guǎn lǐ bàn yè lǐ xǐng lái hū rán kàn jiàn yuàn zi lǐ yǒu
店”的旅馆里。半夜里醒来，忽然看见院子里有

wèi lǎo rén bēi zhe bù dài jiè zhe yuè guāng zhèng zài fān kàn yì běn shū
位老人背着布袋，借着月光正在翻看一本书。

wéi gù hěn hào qí jiù zǒu guò qù xún wèn lǎo rén zài dú shén me shū lǎo rén
韦固很好奇，就走过去询问老人在读什么书。老人

shuō nà běn shū jì zǎi zhe tiān xià nán nǚ de yīn yuán bù dài lǐ de hóng
说，那本书记载着天下男女的姻缘，布袋里的红

shéng shì yòng lái jì zhù yǒu yuán nán nǚ de jiǎo bèi hóng shéng jì zhù jiǎo
绳，是用来系住有缘男女的脚，被红绳系住脚
de nán nǚ huì jié chéng fū qī lǎo rén hái gào su wéi gù tā jiāng lái de
的男女会结成夫妻。老人还告诉韦固，他将来的
qī zi shì cài shì chǎng yí gè fù rén shǒu lǐ bào zhe de xiǎo nǚ hái wéi
妻子是菜市场一个妇人手里抱着的小女孩。韦
gù tīng le hěn bù gāo xìng jué de yí gè nóng fù dài dà de xiǎo nǚ hái gēn
固听了很不高兴，觉得一个农妇带大的小女孩根
běn pèi bú shàng zì jǐ yú shì tā àn zhōng qǐng rén cì shā zhè ge xiǎo
本配不上自己。于是，他暗中请人刺杀这个小
nǚ hái dàn nà cì xíng dòng shī bài le nà rén zhǐ cì shāng le nǚ hái de
女孩，但那次行动失败了，那人只刺伤了女孩的
méi xīn
眉心。

shí jiān guò de hěn kuài duō nián yǐ hòu wéi gù jié hūn le tā
时间过得很快，多年以后，韦固结婚了。他
de qī zi shì xiāng zhōu fǔ guān yuán wáng tài de nǚ ér zhè wèi xiǎo jiě
的妻子是相州府官员王泰的女儿。这位小姐
zhǎng de shí fēn piào liang zhǐ shì méi yǎn zhī jiān cháng cháng tiē gè diàn
长得十分漂亮，只是眉眼之间常常贴个钿
huā wéi gù jué de qí guài biàn wèn tā wèi shén me yào zhè yàng zuò qī
花。韦固觉得奇怪便问她为什么要这样做，妻
zi shuō tā zài nián yòu de shí hou céng bèi qiè zéi cì shāng le méi xīn tiē
子说她在年幼的时候曾被窃贼刺伤了眉心，贴
diàn huā shì wèi zhē gài shāng hén wéi gù tīng le fēi cháng jīng yà xiǎng
钿花是为遮盖伤痕。韦固听了非常惊讶，想
dào nà ge yuè xià lǎo rén de yù yán jìng rán chéng le xiàn shí tā jué de
到那个月下老人的预言竟然成了现实。他觉得
rén shì jiān de nán nǚ yīn yuán shàng tiān zǎo yǐ zhù dìng méi yǒu rén kě
人世间的男女姻缘，上天早已注定，没有人可

yǐ gǎi biàn
以改变。

hòu lái zhè jiàn shì chuán dào le sòng chéng sòng chéng guān yuán jiāng
后来，这件事传到了宋城。宋城官员将

nán diàn tí wéi dìng hūn diàn rén men jiāng zhǎng guǎn yīn yuán de shén chēng
南店题为“定婚店”，人们将掌管姻缘的神称

wéi yuè xià lǎo rén
为“月下老人”。

According to Chinese legend, in the Tang Dynasty, a man named Wei Gu passed the Song City (now Shangqiu, Henan Province) and lived in a hotel called "Nandian". Waking up at midnight, he saw an old man with a cloth bag on his back was reading a book in the moonlight. Wei Gu was curious and came forward to ask what he was reading. The old man told him that this was a book containing the marriages of people in the world and the fates that brought people together. The red threads in the cloth bag were used to tie the feet of the man and woman who were predestined in love and who would be married as a couple. The old man also told Wei Gu that he would marry a little girl who was in the arms of a woman in the food market. Wei Gu was annoyed because he thought a little girl brought up by a peasant woman did not deserve to be his wife. Then he asked a man to kill the little girl. But it failed. The man only hurt the center of the little girl's forehead.

Time passed quickly. Several years later, Wei Gu was married to the daughter of Wang Tai, an official of Xiangzhou. This lady was very beautiful but she always had a twinkle flower decoration in the middle of her forehead. Wei Gu was curious. She told him she was hurt by a thief in the center of her forehead when she was young. To use the twinkle flower decoration was to hide the scar. Wei Gu felt shocked to realize that the prediction of the old man in Nandian came true. He came to know that the marriage between man and woman was predestined by the god and no one could change it.

Later the whole story spread to Song City. Officials in that city renamed Nandian as "Engagement Inn". People called the god who was in charge of marriage "The old man under the moon".

生难字/词注解 | Notes

姻缘：旧时谓婚姻的缘分。

The marriage and fate brings lovers together: The fate of marriage.

钿花：用金、银、玉、贝等做成的花朵状装饰品。

The twinkle flower decoration: Flower-shaped decorations made of gold, silver, jade, and cowry, etc.

故事点评 | Story Comment

月下老人在中国民间是一个家喻户晓的神，他主管着世间男女婚姻，以红绳系在男女脚上定下姻缘。因此，月老是中国文化语境中的爱神，为世人敬奉。

The old man under the moon is a god known by every household. He is in charge of the marriage of men and women by tying red threads on the feet of them to set marriage. Hence，the old man under the moon is the Chinese Cupid who is respected by people.

天仙配

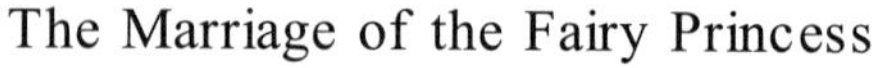

The Marriage of the Fairy Princess

qī xiān nǚ shì yù huáng dà dì de xiǎo nǚ ér tā měi lì shàn liáng yòu
七仙女是玉皇大帝的小女儿，她美丽、善良又
huó pō yì tiān qī xiān nǚ yǔ qí tā jiě mèi cóng tiān gōng zhōng fēi dào rén
活泼。一天，七仙女与其他姐妹从天宫中飞到人
jiān yóu wán dāng tā kàn dào nóng fū zài dì lǐ shī féi gēng zhòng qiáo fū zài
间游玩。当她看到农夫在地里施肥耕种、樵夫在
shān shang kǎn fá chái huo yú fū zài hú lǐ bǔ yú lāo xiā yǐ jí nán nǚ hūn
山上砍伐柴火、渔夫在湖里捕鱼捞虾，以及男女婚
jià shí de rè nao jǐng xiàng zhī hòu duì rén jiān shēng huó chōng mǎn xiàng wǎng
嫁时的热闹景象之后，对人间生活充满向往。

zài rén jiān yóu wán de shí hou qī xiān nǚ ài shàng le yí gè míng jiào
在人间游玩的时候，七仙女爱上了一个名叫
dǒng yǒng de qīng nián tā huí dào tiān gōng yǐ hòu hái jīng cháng tōu tōu de
董永的青年。她回到天宫以后，还经常偷偷地
hé dǒng yǒng xiāng huì hòu lái tā ràng lǎo huái shù zuò wéi tā men de zhèng
和董永相会。后来，她让老槐树作为他们的证

hūn rén liǎng rén bài táng chéng qīn jié hūn yǐ hòu liǎng rén fū chàng fù suí
婚人，两人拜堂成亲。结婚以后，两人夫唱妇随，
shí fēn ēn ài dàn shì méi yǒu guò duō cháng shí jiān zhè jiàn shì qing bèi yù
十分恩爱。但是，没有过多长时间，这件事情被玉
huáng dà dì zhī dào le tā fēi cháng shēng qì mìng lìng qī xiān nǚ lì kè fǎn
皇大帝知道了。他非常生气，命令七仙女立刻返
huí tiān tíng shèn zhì yǐ shā sǐ dǒng yǒng lái wēi xié qī xiān nǚ qī xiān nǚ wèi
回天庭，甚至以杀死董永来威胁七仙女。七仙女为
le dǒng yǒng bú shòu shāng hài zhī hǎo huí dào tiān gōng jiē shòu chéng fá yù
了董永不受伤害，只好回到天宫接受惩罚。玉
huáng dà dì jiāng huái yǒu shēn yùn de qī xiān nǚ qiú jìn zài yún qīng gōng
皇大帝将怀有身孕的七仙女囚禁在云清宫。

guò le bù jiǔ qī xiān nǚ shēng xià le yí gè ér zi yǒu yì tiān
过了不久，七仙女生下了一个儿子。有一天，
yù huáng dà dì dé zhī qī xiān nǚ de hái zi gāng yì chū shēng jiù huì wēi
玉皇大帝得知七仙女的孩子刚一出生就会微
xiào hái bú dào yí gè yuè jiù huì shuō huà yù huáng dà dì duì zhè ge cōng
笑，还不到一个月就会说话。玉皇大帝对这个聪
míng kě ài de hái zi chǎn shēng le shēn hòu de lián ài zhī qíng wáng mǔ
明可爱的孩子产生了深厚的怜爱之情。王母
niáng niang hé qí tā nǚ ér chèn jī zài sān quàn shuō yù huáng dà dì màn
娘娘和其他女儿趁机再三劝说，玉皇大帝慢
màn de gǎi biàn le kàn fǎ tā xià dào rén jiān qīn zì kǎo chá dǒng yǒng de
慢地改变了看法。他下到人间亲自考察董永的
pǐn xíng tā fā xiàn dǒng yǒng qín láo shàn liáng xiào shùn zuì hòu yù
品行。他发现董永勤劳、善良、孝顺。最后，玉
huáng dà dì zhōng yú tóng yì ràng qī xiān nǚ yǔ dǒng yǒng zài rén jiān shēng
皇大帝终于同意让七仙女与董永在人间生
huó chéng quán le tā men de měi hǎo yīn yuán
活，成全了他们的美好姻缘。

The seventh fairy was the little daughter of the Emperor of Heaven. She was beautiful, kind and lively. One day, she flew to the earth from the heavenly palace with her sisters. She saw farmers working in the field, the woodcutters cutting woods in the mountains, the fishers fishing in the lake and the lively scene of people's wedding, which made her yearning for the life on earth.

During their trip on the earth, the seventh fairy fell in love with a young man named Dong Yong. She secretly escaped from the heavenly palace to meet Dong Yong and eventually married to him with an old pagoda tree as their marriage witness. After they married, they became a happy couple like a good Jack makes a good Jill. But not long after, the Emperor of Heaven knew their story, he ordered, even threatened the seventh fairy to return to the heavenly palace instantly, declaring that he would kill Dong Yong if she was against him. To protect Dong Yong, the seventh fairy had to return back to the heavenly palace to accept the punishment, though she was pregnant. She was confined in Yunqing Palace by her father.

Soon, the seventh fairy gave birth to a boy. One day, when the Emperor of Heaven learnt that the child of the seventh fairy could smile from birth and could talk in less than a month, a deep love feeling rose from his heart for this clever and lovely child. The Heaven Queen and other daughters took the advantage of the occasion to persuade the Emperor of Heaven who later changed his mind to go to the earth to get to know the character of Dong Yong. He found Dong Yong was a diligent, kind and filial young man. Finally, he agreed the seventh fairy to live with Dong Yong on the earth, allowing them to lead a happy marriage life.

生难字/词注解 | Note

樵夫：打柴的人。

Woodcutter：A person whose job is to cut down trees.

故事点评 | Story Comment

这是一个古老的爱情故事，七仙女与平凡男子董永之间的爱情，超越天规法令与等级习俗，他们的真情最终感动了玉皇大帝，最后有情人终成眷属。这个故事寄托了人们对婚姻自由与美好生活的向往。

This is an old love story. The love between the seventh fairy and the common person Dong Yong was forbidden by the heaven rules and hierarchical custom. Their love finally moved the Emperor of Heaven. In the end, the lovers led a happy life together, which reflects people's yearning for the freedom of marriage and their pursuit of a beautiful life.

牛郎织女

The Cowherd and the Girl Weaver

hěn jiǔ yǐ qián nán yáng chéng xī bian de niú jiā zhuāng zhù zhe yí
很久以前，南阳城西边的牛家庄，住着一
gè míng jiào niú láng de qīng nián tā zhōng hòu lǎo shi shàn liáng qín kěn
个名叫牛郎的青年。他忠厚老实、善良勤恳，
fù mǔ zài tā hěn xiǎo de shí hou jiù qù shì le tā zhǐ hǎo gēn zhe gē sǎo yì
父母在他很小的时候就去世了，他只好跟着哥嫂一
qǐ shēng huó gē sǎo dài tā shí fēn kè bó píng shí gěi tā gàn zuì kǔ zuì
起生活。哥嫂待他十分刻薄，平时给他干最苦最
lèi de huó niú láng zhǎng dà yǐ hòu hé tā men fēn jiā shí niú láng zhǐ
累的活。牛郎长大以后，和他们分家时，牛郎只
fēn dào le yì tóu nián lǎo de niú hé yí liàng pò chē
分到了一头年老的牛和一辆破车。

niú láng hé lǎo niú xiāng yī wéi mìng　tā men zhù zài máo cǎo fáng lǐ
牛郎和老牛相依为命。他们住在茅草房里，
píng shí zài shān shàng kāi kěn huāng dì　gēng zhòng liáng shi　rì zi guò de hěn
平时在山上开垦荒地，耕种粮食，日子过得很
jiān nán　yì tiān　lǎo niú tū rán kāi kǒu shuō huà le　gào su tā bì lián chí
艰难。一天，老牛突然开口说话了，告诉他碧莲池
yǒu xiān nǚ zài xǐ zǎo　yào tā bǎ nà jiàn hóng sè de yī fu cáng qǐ lái　nà
有仙女在洗澡，要他把那件红色的衣服藏起来，那
ge xiān nǚ jiù huì chéng wéi tā de qī zi　niú láng tīng shuō hòu yòu jīng qí
个仙女就会成为他的妻子。牛郎听说后又惊奇
yòu gāo xìng　guǒ zhēn dào bì lián chí ná zǒu le nà jiàn hóng sè de yī fu
又高兴，果真到碧莲池拿走了那件红色的衣服。
nà jiàn hóng sè yī fu shì zhī nǚ de　zhī nǚ jiù zhè yàng chéng le niú láng de
那件红色衣服是织女的，织女就这样成了牛郎的
qī zi
妻子。

tā men hūn hòu de rì zi guò de měi mǎn xìng fú　hái shēng xià le yì
他们婚后的日子过得美满幸福，还生下了一
ér yì nǚ　hòu lái　zhè jiàn shì qing bèi wáng mǔ niáng niang zhī dào le　tā
儿一女。后来，这件事情被王母娘娘知道了，她
duì zhī nǚ méi yǒu jīng yǔn xǔ jiù hé niú láng jié hūn shēng zǐ　fēi cháng fèn
对织女没有经允许就和牛郎结婚生子，非常愤
nù　tā pài qiǎn tiān bīng tiān jiàng qù zhuā bǔ zhī nǚ huí lái jiē shòu
怒。她派遣天兵天将去抓捕织女回来接受
chéng fá
惩罚。

zhī nǚ bèi zhuā zǒu le　niú láng hěn jiāo jí　zài lǎo niú de zhǐ diǎn
织女被抓走了，牛郎很焦急。在老牛的指点
xià　tā chuān shàng niú pí zuò de xié　yòng luó kuāng tiāo zhe yí duì ér nǚ
下，他穿上牛皮做的鞋，用箩筐挑着一对儿女，

fēi shàng yún tiān qù zhuī gǎn zhī nǚ yǎn kàn jiù kuài yào zhuī shàng de shí
飞上云天去追赶织女。眼看就快要追上的时
hou wáng mǔ niáng niang bá xià tóu shang de jīn zān wǎng tiān kōng zhōng yì
候，王母娘娘拔下头上的金簪往天空中一
huá dùn shí yì tiáo tiān hé chū xiàn zài zhī nǚ hé niú láng zhōng jiān niú láng
划，顿时一条天河出现在织女和牛郎中间。牛郎
zài yě zhuī bú shàng zhī nǚ le tā men xiāng hù jiào zhe duì fāng de míng
再也追不上织女了，他们相互叫着对方的名
zi ér nǚ men dà shēng kū hǎn zhe mā ma zhè yì bēi cǎn de chǎng
字，儿女们大声哭喊着“妈妈”。这一悲惨的场
jǐng gǎn dòng le qiān wàn zhī xǐ què tā men fēi guò lái dā chéng yí zuò
景，感动了千万只喜鹊，它们飞过来，搭成一座
què qiáo ràng tā men zǒu shàng què qiáo xiāng huì zhè yì tiān zhèng hǎo shì qī
鹊桥，让他们走上鹊桥相会。这一天正好是七
yuè chū qī wáng mǔ niáng niang dā ying měi nián de zhè ge shí hou tā men kě
月初七，王母娘娘答应每年的这个时候，他们可
yǐ zài què qiáo xiāng huì
以在鹊桥相会。

chuán shuō cóng cǐ yǐ hòu měi nián nóng lì de qī yuè qī rì niú
传说从此以后，每年农历的七月七日，牛
láng zhī nǚ hé ér nǚ men jiù huì gé zhe tiān hé zài què qiáo shang xiāng huì
郎、织女和儿女们就会隔着天河在鹊桥上相会，
qīn mì de shuō zhe qiāo qiāo huà
亲密地说着悄悄话。

Long time ago, in the Niu Village in the west of Nanyang City, there lived a young cowherd named Niulang who was kind, simple-hearted and hard-working whose parents died when he was a little boy. He had to live with his brother and sister-in-law who treated him tartly and meanly by giving him the most dirty and tiring work to do. When he grew up to be able to divide up the family property descended from the parents and live apart from his brother and sister-in-law, he was given only an old cattle and a broken cart.

Mutually depended upon each other for survival, Niulang and the old cattle lived in a thatched house. They reclaimed and cultivated field and planted food. Things were tough for them. One day, the old cattle began to talk and told him a fairy was having her bath in the Bilian Pool. He could hide the red clothes and its owner would be his wife. Niulang was surprised and happy to hear that. He came to the Bilian Pool for the red clothes whose owner was the Girl Weaver who did become Niulang's wife later.

After they were married, they had a happy life with a son and a daughter. The Heaven Queen was so furious when she knew the Girl Weaver was married without permission that she sent divine troops descending from heaven to capture the Girl Weaver to punish her.

The cowherd was anxious to see the Girl Weaver being taken away. Under the advice of the old cattle, he wore shoes made of cowhide and carried his children in a pair of large bamboo baskets, flying to chase the Girl Weaver. At the time when he was about to catch up, the Heaven Queen took off her golden hairpin and waved it in the sky. Instantly, a river, the Milky Way, was drawn out to separate the couple. The cowherd could never chase up his wife. They called each other's name and their children cried loudly for mother. The sad scene moved thousands of magpies who flew to make a bridge over the Milky Way, on which the cowherd and the Girl Weaver came together for reunion. It was the seventh day of lunar July. The heaven queen agreed each year on that day, they could meet each other on the bridge formed by magpies.

According to Chinese legend, each year on the seventh day of lunar July, the cowherd and the Girl Weaver as well as their children would have their reunion: they looked at each other with strong emotion and whispered to each other intimately.

生难字/词注解 | Notes

刻薄：待人处事挑剔、无情。

Tartly and meanly: Treating others in a picky and cold manner.

簪：用来绾住头发的一种首饰。

Hairpin: A small thin piece of wire that is folded in the middle, used by women to hold their hair in place.

顿时：极短的时间。

Instantly: Happening in a very short time.

故事点评 | Story Comment

牛郎织女鹊桥相会是一个美丽动人的爱情故事，是我国四大民间爱情传说之一，享有很高的声誉。现在每年农历七月初七，姑娘们就会仰望星空，乞求上天赐予美满婚姻，由此形成了“七夕节”，亦名“乞巧节”。

The story of the cowherd and the Girl Weaver having their reunion on the bridge formed by magpies is a beautiful and touching love story which is popular as one of the four Chinese folk love legends. When it comes to the seventh of lunar July, girls would look up in the sky to wish for a good marriage. This day has become a festival called Qixi Festival or Qiqiao Festival, the Chinese Valentine's Day.

孟姜女哭长城

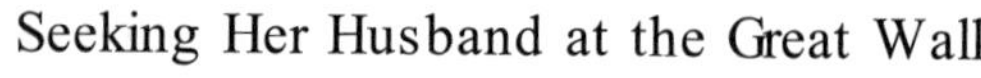

Seeking Her Husband at the Great Wall

xiāng chuán zài qín shǐ huáng tǒng zhì shí qī qīng zhuàng nián dà bù fen
相传在秦始皇统治时期，青壮年大部分
dōu bèi pò lí kāi jiā xiāng qù yáo yuǎn de dì fang zuò hěn fán zhòng de láo
都被迫离开家乡去遥远的地方做很繁重的劳
yì qīng nián fàn xǐ liáng wèi duǒ bì bèi zhuā qù zuò láo yì jiù sì chù
役。青年范喜良为躲避被抓去做劳役，就四处
táo nàn
逃难。

zhè yì tiān guān bīng zhèng zài zhuā rén fàn xǐ liáng hěn jīng huāng tā
这一天官兵正在抓人，范喜良很惊慌。他
jiù zài fù jìn yí hù rén jiā de huā yuán zhōng duǒ qǐ lái zhè hù rén jiā
就在附近一户人家的花园中躲起来。这户人家
xìng mèng mèng jiā yǒu yí gè nǚ ér jiào mèng jiāng nǚ rén zhǎng de piào
姓孟，孟家有一个女儿叫孟姜女，人长得漂

liang hái hěn cōng míng zhè tiān mèng jiāng nǚ zhèng zài yuán zhōng wán shuǎ
亮，还很聪明。这天孟姜女正在园中玩耍，
qià qiǎo pèng jiàn fàn xǐ liáng liǎng gè rén xiāng hù ài mù děng guān bīng
恰巧碰见范喜良，两个人相互爱慕。等官兵
zǒu hòu jiù yóu mèng jiāng nǚ de fù qīn zuò wéi zhèng hūn rén liǎng rén jié le
走后，就由孟姜女的父亲作为证婚人，两人结了
hūn kě shì xīn hūn gāng guò le sān tiān fàn xǐ liáng hái shì bèi guān bīng
婚。可是，新婚刚过了三天，范喜良还是被官兵
zhuā zǒu le bèi yā qù xiū zhù cháng chéng hòu lái fàn xǐ liáng jīn bú zhù
抓走了，被押去修筑长城。后来，范喜良禁不住
fán zhòng de tǐ lì láo dòng bù jiǔ jiù láo lèi guò dù lèi sǐ le shī gǔ
繁重的体力劳动，不久就劳累过度，累死了，尸骨
bèi suí biàn de yǎn mái zài cháng chéng qiáng xià
被随便地掩埋在长城墙下。

dōng tiān dào le xià zhe dà xuě mèng jiāng nǚ zài jiā lǐ shí fēn diàn
冬天到了，下着大雪，孟姜女在家里十分惦
jì zhàng fu tā xiǎng tiān qì zhè me hán lěng zhàng fu xiū zhù cháng
记丈夫。她想，天气这么寒冷，丈夫修筑长
chéng què méi yǒu hòu shi de yī fu chuān yú shì tā féng zhì hǎo yí jiàn
城却没有厚实的衣服穿。于是，她缝制好一件
mián yī dài zài shēn shang lì jìn jiān nán zǒu le qiān lǐ de lù chéng lái
棉衣带在身上，历尽艰难，走了千里的路程来
xún zhǎo zhàng fu zhè yì tiān tā zhōng yú lái dào cháng chéng biān shang
寻找丈夫。这一天，她终于来到长城边上。
méi yǒu xiǎng dào dé dào de què shì zhàng fu yǐ jīng lèi sǐ de xiāo xi tā
没有想到得到的却是丈夫已经累死的消息。她
fēi cháng bēi shāng zài nà lǐ kū de tiān hūn dì àn hū rán zhǐ tīng jiàn
非常悲伤，在那里哭得天昏地暗。忽然，只听见
huā lā yì shēng jù xiǎng cháng chéng dǎo tā le bā bǎi lǐ lù chū fàn
“哗啦”一声巨响，长城倒塌了八百里，露出范

xǐ liáng de hái gǔ
喜良的骸骨。

zhè jiàn shì qing jīng dòng le qín shǐ huáng tā xià lìng zhuō ná mèng jiāng
这件事情惊动了秦始皇，他下令捉拿孟姜
nǚ wèn zuì kě shì dāng qín shǐ huáng kàn jiàn mèng jiāng nǚ shí jiàn tā
女问罪。可是，当秦始皇看见孟姜女时，见她
zhǎng xiàng měi mào jiù xiǎng yào nà tā wéi pín fēi mèng jiāng nǚ jiān jué
长相美貌，就想要纳她为嫔妃。孟姜女坚决
bù dā ying bù xī yǐ sǐ lái jù jué dàn shì tā xīn xiǎng zhàng fu hán
不答应，不惜以死来拒绝。但是，她心想丈夫含
hèn ér sǐ hái méi yǒu bào chóu zì jǐ zěn me néng zhè yàng bái bái sǐ qù
恨而死，还没有报仇，自己怎么能这样白白死去
ne yú shì tā jiǎ zhuāng tóng yì jié hūn dàn bì xū xiān dā ying tā sān
呢？于是，她假装同意结婚，但必须先答应她三
gè tiáo jiàn yī shì yào wèi zhàng fu xiū fén lì bēi èr shì yào huáng dì pī
个条件：一是要为丈夫修坟立碑；二是要皇帝披
má dài xiào qīn zì jì diàn sān shì zài hǎi biān jǔ xíng hūn lǐ qín shǐ huáng
麻戴孝亲自祭奠；三是在海边举行婚礼。秦始皇
quán bù dā ying le zuì hòu sān jiàn shì quán bù zuò wán qín shǐ huáng yǐ
全部答应了。最后，三件事全部做完，秦始皇以
wéi xīn yuàn dé chéng le méi yǒu xiǎng dào gāng liè de mèng jiāng nǚ què bào
为心愿得成了。没有想到刚烈的孟姜女却抱
zhe zhàng fu de yí gǔ tiào jìn le dà hǎi
着丈夫的遗骨，跳进了大海。

According to Chinese legend, in the Qin Dynasty, most young male adults were forced to go to distant places to do hard work away from hometown. A young man named Fan Xiliang fled to escape from being a forced labor.

One day, seeing officials and soldiers arresting people for labors, Fan Xiliang felt panic and hid in a garden of one house nearby. This garden belonged to a family named Meng who had a daughter named Meng Jiangnü, a beautiful and clever lady. On that day, Meng Jiangnü was playing in the garden and encountered Fan Xiliang there. Later they fell in love with each other. After those officials and soldiers left, they married to each other with the lady's father as their wedding witness. But, only three days after the wedding, Fan Xiliang was finally caught by the officials and soldiers and sent to build the Great Wall. Later, Fan Xiliang died for he could not stand the heavy labor work. His body was buried under the Great Wall carelessly .

Winter came, it snowed heavily. Meng Jiangnü missed her husband greatly. She sewed a cotton padded coat for her husband thinking he only had thin clothes to wear in the cold weather. Suffering all kinds of hardships, she travelled thousands of *li* to find her husband before she arrived at the Great Wall. Unexpectedly she got the bad news that her husband had already died of tiredness. She felt sorrowful and cried heartbreakingly till she heard one big loud crashing sound caused by the collapsing of the Great Wall in eight hundred *li* under which she saw her husband's corpse.

The news startled the First Emperor of Qin who ordered his army to arrest Meng Jiangnü. But when the First Emperor of Qin saw the beautiful Meng Jiangnü, he changed his mind and wanted to make her his concubine. Meng Jiangnü firmly refused even at the price of death. But when she thought of her husband's death, she wanted to survive for revenge. So, she pretended to agree to the marriage but firstly the First Emperor of Qin should agree with her on three conditions. First, her husband should be buried with a grave and a tombstone. Second, the emperor should dress in mourning to hold a memorial ceremony for her husband. Third, the wedding should be held by the sea. All were agreed by the First Emperor of Qin. Finally, after the three things were done, the First Emperor of Qin thought he would marry Meng Jiangnü as he expected. Out of his expectation, the strong-minded Meng Jiangnü jumped into the sea with the remains of her husband.

生难字/词注解 | Notes

劳役：指统治者强迫人民出劳力当差服役。

Forced labor: People forced to be labor without payment by the governor.

倒塌：崩塌。

Collapse: To fall down or fall in suddenly, often after breaking apart.

骸骨：即尸骨、尸体。

Corpse: A dead body, especially of a human.

祭奠：为追念死者而举行仪式祭奠亡魂。

Hold a memorial ceremony for: Hold a memorial ceremony to remember the dead.

故事点评 | Story Comment

孟姜女哭倒长城的故事在中国民间流传广泛，妇孺皆知。这一故事展露了孟姜女对爱情的坚贞不渝和对统治者的反抗精神。后人在山海关建了姜女庙，以表达对孟姜女的哀悼与纪念。

The story of Meng Jiangnü who cried and caused the collapse of the Great Wall, is popular among the people. It is well-known by the people. This story showed her loyal love to her husband and her rebellious spirit to the ruler. The descendents built Jiangnü Temple at Shanhai Pass to grieve over her death and commemorate her.

嫦娥奔月

The Goddess Chang'e's Ascending to the Moon

chuán shuō yì shì shàng gǔ shí qī de shè rì yīng xióng yīn wèi dé zuì
传说羿是上古时期的射日英雄，因为得罪
le tiān dì suǒ yǐ bèi biǎn zhé dào rén jiān zuò le yí gè píng fán de rén
了天帝，所以被贬谪到人间做了一个平凡的人。
yì píng shí yǐ dǎ liè wéi chí shēng huó yīn wèi shēng huó pín kǔ yì hěn cán
羿平时以打猎维持生活。因为生活贫苦，羿很惭
kuì jué de duì bú zhù qī zi cháng é zǒng shì xiǎng zhe néng gòu duì qī zi
愧，觉得对不住妻子嫦娥，总是想着能够对妻子
yǒu suǒ bǔ cháng
有所补偿。

yú shì yì jīng guò cháng tú bá shè zài kūn lún shān xī wáng mǔ nà
于是，羿经过长途跋涉，在昆仑山西王母那

lǐ qiú dào le yì zhǒng kě yǐ cháng shēng bù sǐ de yào wán yì hé xī
里求到了一种可以长生不死的药丸。羿和西

wáng mǔ gào bié de shí hou xī wáng mǔ zài sān zhǔ fù yào wán ruò fēn gěi
王母告别的时候，西王母再三嘱咐，药丸若分给

liǎng gè rén chī kě yǐ cháng shēng bù sǐ rú guǒ yí gè rén chī jiù huì fēi
两个人吃可以长生不死，如果一个人吃就会飞

shàng tiān chéng wéi shén xiān yì shě bù dé dú zì yí gè rén chī xià qù
上天成为神仙。羿舍不得独自一个人吃下去。

huí jiā hòu jiù bǎ yào wán jiāo gěi cháng é bǎo guǎn liǎng rén shāng liang hǎo dì
回家后就把药丸交给嫦娥保管，两人商量好第

èr tiān yì qǐ chī xià qù cháng é kàn dào yì ná dào cháng shēng bù sǐ de
二天一起吃下去。嫦娥看到羿拿到长生不死的

xiān yào xīn lǐ shí fēn gāo xìng
仙药，心里十分高兴。

dāng tiān wǎn shang yì shuì zháo le xīn qíng jī dòng de cháng é què
当天晚上，羿睡着了，心情激动的嫦娥却

zěn me yě shuì bù zháo tā jīn bú zhù qǐ shēn chá kàn xiān yào tā yì biān
怎么也睡不着。她禁不住起身查看仙药，她一边

kàn zhe yì biān huí yì dāng nián tā zuò shén xiān shí de zì yóu yǔ kuài huo
看着，一边回忆当年她做神仙时的自由与快活。

kě shì xiàn zài shēng huó què zhè yàng jiān nán cháng é kāi shǐ mán yuàn yì
可是，现在生活却这样艰难，嫦娥开始埋怨羿

le tā zài yě bù xiǎng guò zhè zhǒng shēng huó yú shì tā háo bù yóu yù
了，她再也不想过这种生活。于是，她毫不犹豫

de tūn xià yào wán zhè shí qí jì fā shēng le cháng é gǎn jué shēn
地吞下药丸。这时，奇迹发生了。嫦娥感觉身

tǐ qīng piāo piāo de bù zhī bù jué fēi xiàng chuāng wài zhí shàng yún tiān
体轻飘飘的，不知不觉飞向窗外，直上云天。

rán ér cháng é yǔ yì bì jìng fū qī yì chǎng tā xīn lǐ réng rán shí fēn
然而，嫦娥与羿毕竟夫妻一场，她心里仍然十分

guà niàn yì yú shì tā jiù zài lí rén jiān zuì jìn de yuè gōng zhōng tíng le
挂念羿。于是，她就在离人间最近的月宫中停了
xià lái
下来。

cháng é bēn xiàng yuè gōng hòu yì fēi cháng shāng xīn yǒu yì nián
嫦娥奔向月宫后，羿非常伤心。有一年
qià féng bā yuè shí wǔ tā fā xiàn nà wǎn de yuè liang tè bié míng liàng
恰逢八月十五，他发现那晚的月亮特别明亮。
yì hěn sī niàn qī zi yú shì yì jiù zài yuàn zi lǐ bǎi shàng xiāng àn
羿很思念妻子，于是，羿就在院子里摆上香案，
zài xiāng àn shàng miàn fàng le cháng é píng shí ài chī de guā guǒ lái jì bài
在香案上面放了嫦娥平时爱吃的瓜果来祭拜
tā cóng cǐ měi nián dào le nóng lì de bā yuè shí wǔ rén men dōu huì
她。从此，每年到了农历的八月十五，人们都会
jìn xíng lóng zhòng de bài yuè lǐ yí zhè yì fēng sú dài dài xiāng chuán hòu
进行隆重的拜月礼仪。这一风俗代代相传，后
lái chéng le zhōng huá mín zú de chuán tǒng jié rì zhōng qiū jié
来成了中华民族的传统节日——中秋节。

According to Chinese legend, in ancient times, Yi was a hero for shooting down the suns but he offended the Emperor of Heaven who relegated him to a common people. Yi supported his life by hunting. Because of the poor life, Yi felt guilty for his wife Chang'e. He always wanted to find ways to compensate.

He travelled hundreds and thousands of *li* to the Kunlun

Mountain where the Queen Mother of the West lived for the elixir of life. Before departing with the Queen Mother of the West, he was enjoined repeatedly that this pill should be halved and taken by two persons for immortality. If it was taken by only one person, that person would fly up to the heaven and become a god. Yi was reluctant to have it alone. He went home and gave the pill to Chang'e and decided to have it together with her the next day. Chang'e was delighted to see that Yi had brought back the elixir of life.

On that night, Yi was asleep while Chang'e was too excited to fall in sleep. She could not help to check the pill. She recalled the happy and free life she had when she was a fairy while the present life here was tough. She began to complain and never wanted to have this kind of life again. Then she took the pill alone unconsciously. A miracle happened. Chang'e felt herself light and began to fly to the window and all the way to the heaven. However, Chang'e missed her husband very much, and then she stopped at the Moon Palace which was the nearest one from the earth.

After Chang'e flew to the Moon Palace, Yi felt sad and missed his wife greatly. One year when it came to the lunar August 15th, he found the moon extremely bright. Then he set an incense table and put her favorite fruits to commemorate his wife. Since then, each year, when it came to the lunar 15th August, people would hold a grand ceremony to worship the moon, which was descended from generations to generations. It turned to be one of the traditional Chinese festivals—Mid-Autumn Day.

生难字/词注解 | Note

贬谪：官吏降职并调往远方就任。

Relegate: To give somebody a lower or less important position, rank, etc. than before or transfer somebody to a distant place.

故事点评 | Story Comment

嫦娥奔月是一个美丽动人的神话，展现嫦娥超越平凡生活，追求自由的精神。在民间，每年农历八月十五日，这天的月亮比其他时候更圆，更明亮。因此，中秋节又称"团圆节"，象征着家人团圆、安乐与幸福。

The story of Chang'e who flew to the Moon Palace is a touching myth. It shows her spirit of pursuing free life which went beyond the ordinary life. Among the folk, each year, when it comes to the lunar 15th August, the moon is extremely brighter. Mid-Autumn Day is called "reunion festival" which means reunion, peace and happiness.

沉香救母

Chenxiang Rescuing His Mother

hàn cháo shí yǒu yí gè shū shēng míng jiào liú xǐ yǒu yì nián tā
汉朝时，有一个书生名叫刘玺。有一年他
jìn jīng qù cān jiā kǎo shì lù guò huà shān sān shèng mǔ shén miào shí duì sān
进京去参加考试，路过华山三圣母神庙时，对三
shèng mǔ de yàn lì róng yán hěn ài mù qíng bú zì jīn de tí le yì shǒu qíng
圣母的艳丽容颜很爱慕，情不自禁地题了一首情
shī zài qiáng bì shang sān shèng mǔ zhī dào hòu hěn shēng qì rèn wéi shì
诗在墙壁上。三圣母知道后，很生气，认为是
mào fàn le tā de wēi yán dǎ suàn chéng fá yí xià liú xǐ hòu lái què bèi
冒犯了她的威严，打算惩罚一下刘玺，后来却被
liú xǐ de zhēn chéng gǎn dòng liǎng rén sī zì jié wéi fū qī
刘玺的真诚感动，两人私自结为夫妻。

hūn hòu sān tiān liú xǐ yào qù cān jiā kǎo shì le tā zǒu de shí hou
婚后三天，刘玺要去参加考试了。他走的时候

zèng sòng sān shèng mǔ yí kuài chén xiāng dīng zhǔ rú guǒ huái yùn shēng le hái
赠送三圣母一块沉香，叮嘱如果怀孕生了孩
zi yào gěi hái zi qǔ chén xiāng wéi míng kě shì liǎng rén sī zì jié
子，要给孩子取“沉香”为名。可是，两人私自结
hūn de shì qing bèi sān shèng mǔ de gē ge èr láng shén zhī dào le tā fēi
婚的事情被三圣母的哥哥二郎神知道了，他非
cháng fèn nù yào zhuō ná tā shàng tiān qù jiē shòu chǔ fá èr láng shén xiān
常愤怒，要捉拿她上天去接受处罚。二郎神先
tōu zǒu sān shèng mǔ de fǎ bǎo bǎo lián dēng jiē zhe jiāng sān shèng mǔ
偷走三圣母的法宝——宝莲灯，接着将三圣母
kòu yā zài huà shān jiǎo xià
扣押在华山脚下。

hòu lái sān shèng mǔ zài dòng xué zhōng shēng xià hái zi qǔ míng jiào
后来，三圣母在洞穴中生下孩子，取名叫
chén xiāng tā tuō fù yè cha jiāng chén xiāng sòng chū qù bài shī xué yì
沉香。她托付夜叉将沉香送出去拜师学艺。
zài shén xiān zhǐ dǎo xià chén xiāng xué huì le shàng bǎi zhǒng wǔ yì hái huì
在神仙指导下，沉香学会了上百种武艺，还会
qī shí èr zhǒng biàn huà dào tā shí liù suì de shí hou chén xiāng gào bié
七十二种变化。到他十六岁的时候，沉香告别
shī fu shuō yào qù huà shān jiù chū bèi yā de mǔ qīn shī fu zèng gěi tā yì
师父，说要去华山救出被压的母亲，师父赠给他一
bǐng míng wéi xuān huā de shén fǔ
柄名为“萱花”的神斧。

chén xiāng lái dào huà shān qǐng qiú jiù jiu èr láng shén shì fàng mǔ qīn
沉香来到华山，请求舅舅二郎神释放母亲，
èr láng shén què bù dā ying yú shì liǎng rén zhǎn kāi dà zhàn dǎ le jǐ
二郎神却不答应。于是，两人展开大战，打了几
bǎi huí hé hòu bù fēn shèng fù gè lù shén xiān yǒu de tóng qíng chén
百回合后，不分胜负。各路神仙有的同情沉

xiāng yǒu de zé shuō èr láng shén yǒu lǐ tā men fēn chéng liǎng pài yí
香，有的则说二郎神有理。他们分成两派，一

pài bāng zhù chén xiāng lìng yí pài zé bāng zhù èr láng shén jù shuō dāng
派帮助沉香，另一派则帮助二郎神。据说，当

shí liǎng pài shén xiān dòu fǎ shā de dì dòng shān yáo tiān hūn dì àn
时两派神仙斗法，杀得地动山摇，天昏地暗。

zhè jiàn shì zuì hòu jīng dòng yù huáng dà dì tā mìng lìng tài bái jīn xīng
这件事最后惊动玉皇大帝，他命令太白金星

qián lái shuō hé bìng yǐ fǎ lì fēn kāi zhòng shén chén xiāng chèn jī yòng
前来说和，并以法力分开众神。沉香趁机用

shén fǔ pī kāi le huà shān jiù chū sān shèng mǔ mǔ zǐ dé yǐ tuán jù
神斧劈开了华山，救出三圣母，母子得以团聚。

In the Han Dynasty, there was a scholar named Liu Xi who went to the capital of the country to attend the imperial examination. On his way there, he passed the Sanshengmu Temple in the Hua Mountain. He adored the statue of Sanshengmu for her beautiful look. Then he wrote a love poem on the wall. After learning it, Sanshengmu was very angry for thinking Liu Xi offended her holy statue and decided to punish him. But later she was moved by the sincerity of Liu Xi and married him.

Three days after marriage, Liu Xi went to attend the exam. Before departing with Sanshengmu, he sent her a piece of eaglewood and repeatedly advised if she got pregnant, she should name the baby "Chenxiang". But their marriage was known by Sanshengmu's brother, Erlang Shen, who was so angry that he wanted to take his sister back to the heaven for punishment. Erlang Shen stole the magic weapon of his sister—Lotus Lantern. Then he confined his sister at the foot of the Hua Mountain.

Later, Sanshengmu gave birth to a baby and called him Chenxiang. She asked Yecha (Yaksa) for help to send her baby to masters to learn skills. With the guidance of gods, Chenxiang learnt hundreds of martial skills including seventy-two metamorphoses. In the year when Chenxiang was sixteen, in order to rescue his mother from the Hua Mountain, Chenxiang departed with his master who sent him a holy axe called Xuanhua.

After arriving at the Hua Mountain, Chenxiang pleaded to his uncle to set his mother free. But Erlang Shen refused. Then they started to fight. After hundreds of rounds' fighting, there was still no winner. Some of the gods felt sympathy for Chenxiang and helped him, while others thought Erlang Shen was right and supported him. In Chinese legend, all the gods were fighting fiercely showing their own magic arts.

Then the Emperor of Heaven ordered Taibai Jinxing to persuade each party to stop and use magic arts to separate all the gods, while Chenxiang took advantage of the chance to separate the Hua Mountain and rescued his mother out with the holy axe. The mother and the son finally reunited with each other.

生难字/词注解 | Notes

刘玺：人名。
Liu Xi： The name of a man.

惩罚：严厉的惩戒或处罚。
Punish： To make somebody suffer because they have broken the law or done something wrong.

夜叉：鬼神名。
Yecha (Yaksa)： The name of some supernatural beings.

故事点评 | Story Comment

沉香为救母亲，不畏艰难险阻，展露他的一片赤诚孝敬之心。他的孝心感动了神仙，在神仙的帮助下，母子团圆。这个故事告诉我们要敢于冲破阻挠，坚定目标，付出行动，总有一天会取得成功。

Regardless of all the difficulties and obstacles, Chenxiang tried his best to rescue his mother, which showed his filial love that moved the gods with whose help he reunited with his mother. This story tells us we should be brave to break obstacles. With a firm aim, once we take actions, we would achieve success.

哪吒闹海

Prince Nezha's Triumph Against Dragon King

chén táng guān zǒng bīng lǐ jìng de fū rén huái tāi sān nián líng liù gè yuè
陈塘关总兵李靖的夫人怀胎三年零六个月

hòu yǒu yì tiān shēng xià yí gè ròu qiú lǐ tiān wáng hěn jīng yà jué de
后，有一天生下一个肉球。李天王很惊讶，觉得

zhè shì bù jí xiáng de yù zhào yú shì tā yòng jiàn bǎ ròu qiú pī kāi
这是不吉祥的预兆。于是，他用剑把肉球劈开，

hū rán guāng máng sì shè ròu qiú zhōng tiào chū yí gè huó pō kě ài de xiǎo
忽然光芒四射，肉球中跳出一个活泼可爱的小

nán hái
男孩。

jiā lǐ fā shēng zhè zhǒng qí guài de shì qing lǐ jìng xīn qíng hěn yù
家里发生这种奇怪的事情，李靖心情很郁

mèn yí wèi míng jiào tài yǐ zhēn rén de dào zhǎng què lái hè xǐ wèi zhè ge
闷。一位名叫太乙真人的道长却来贺喜，为这个

xiǎo nán hái qǔ míng wéi né zhā bìng shōu tā wéi tú dì zèng sòng tā liǎng jiàn
小男孩取名为哪吒，并收他为徒弟，赠送他两件
bǎo wù qián kūn quān hé hún tiān líng
宝物：乾坤圈和混天绫。

né zhā qī suì de shí hou fā shēng hàn zāi dōng hǎi lóng wáng bù jǐn
哪吒七岁的时候，发生旱灾。东海龙王不仅
bú jiàng yǔ lái jiù zāi ér qiě hái mìng lìng yè chā qù hǎi biān qiǎng duó shào
不降雨来救灾，而且还命令夜叉去海边抢夺少
nán shào nǚ né zhā fēi cháng fèn nù tā yòng qián kūn quān dǎ sǐ yè chā
男少女。哪吒非常愤怒，他用乾坤圈打死夜叉，
yòu shā le qián lái jiù yuán de lóng wáng ér zi áo bǐng lóng wáng qù yù
又杀了前来救援的龙王儿子敖丙。龙王去玉
huáng dà dì nà lǐ gào zhuàng yě zāo dào né zhā yí dùn hěn dǎ yú shì
皇大帝那里告状，也遭到哪吒一顿狠打。于是，
dōng hǎi lóng wáng qǐng lái qí tā sān wèi lóng wáng xiōng dì shāng tǎo duì cè
东海龙王请来其他三位龙王兄弟，商讨对策。

dì èr tiān sì hǎi lóng wáng dài lǐng shuǐ bīng shuǐ jiàng xiān qǐ jù làng
第二天，四海龙王带领水兵水将掀起巨浪，
bǎ chén táng guān yān mò le lóng wáng bī pò lǐ jìng jiāo chū né zhā né
把陈塘关淹没了。龙王逼迫李靖交出哪吒。哪
zhā xiǎng yào yíng zhàn fǎn jī zāo dào fù qīn de zǔ lán lǐ jìng hái bǎ né
吒想要迎战反击，遭到父亲的阻拦，李靖还把哪
zhā de liǎng jiàn fǎ bǎo gěi mò shōu le
吒的两件法宝给没收了。

né zhā wèi le fù mǔ hé quán chéng bǎi xìng de ān wēi hěn bēi fèn
哪吒为了父母和全城百姓的安危，很悲愤
de zì shā le tài yǐ zhēn rén zhī dào né zhā de yǒng gǎn hé rén yì
地自杀了。太乙真人知道哪吒的勇敢和仁义
hòu jiè hé yè hé huā de jīng qì shǐ né zhā qǐ sǐ huí shēng xīn
后，借荷叶、荷花的精气使哪吒起死回生。新

shēng hòu de né zhā shǒu chí huǒ jiān qiāng jiǎo tà fēng huǒ lún dà nào dōng
生后的哪吒手持火尖枪、脚踏风火轮，大闹东

hǎi lóng gōng huó zhuō le lóng wáng shǐ lóng wáng jiē shòu le yīng yǒu de
海龙宫，活捉了龙王，使龙王接受了应有的

chéng fá
惩罚。

Chentang Pass military commander Li Jing's wife has been pregnant for three years and six months and gave a birth to a flesh ball finally. Li Jing was shocked, believing it to be a bad omen, and halved the meat ball with his sword. All of a sudden, a flash of light radiated in all directions, from the flesh ball jumped a lovely little boy.

Li Jing felt gloomy with this strange thing but a Taoist priest named Taiyi Zhenren came around for congratulations and named the little boy Nezha. He accepted Nezha as his apprentice and sent him two magic weapons: Qiankun Quan and Huntian Ling.

When Nezha was seven years old, drought happened. Dragon King of the East Sea not only did not make rainfall to save people from the natural disaster but also ordered Yecha to rob little boys and girls by the sea. With his Qiankun Quan, Nezha furiously killed both Yecha and Aobing (son of the Dragon King) who came around for rescue. Dragon King of the East Sea complained to the Emperor of Heaven but he was also beaten fiercely by Nezha. Then he invited the other three brothers to discuss for tactics.

The next day, the four Dragon Kings led their marines to arouse huge waves, flooding Chentang Pass and threatening Li Jing to hand over Nezha who still wanted to fight back. But Li Jing stopped Nezha and took away two magic weapons from him.

For the safety of people in the city, Nezha suicided in indignation. After learning Nezha's braveness, kindheartedness and justice, Taiyi Zhenren resurrected him by the vital essence of lotus leaves and lotus flowers. With Fire-tipped Spear in hand, Wind Fire Wheels on feet, the reborn Nezha went to fight in the East Sea Dragon Palace and caught the Dragon King of the East Sea. The Dragon King received the due punishment.

生难字/词注解 | Note

李靖：天宫中的托塔李天王。

Li Jing: The God of the heavenly palace who carries a tower in hand.

| Story Comment

在这个故事中，哪吒展露出他的善良、坚强与勇敢。他面对强大敌人，毫不示弱，为了百姓，他又甘愿接受处罚。哪吒的不畏强权与天真烂漫，备受后人喜爱。

In this story, Nezha showed his kindness, adamancy and doughtiness. Faced with strong enemies, he did not show any fear. For the safety of the common people, he bravely accepted punishment. Nezha is loved by the descendents for he never feared power and also for his naïvety.

八仙过海

The Eight Immortals Crossing the Sea

chuán shuō tiě guǎi lǐ hàn zhōng lí lán cǎi hé zhāng guǒ lǎo hé
传说铁拐李、汉钟离、蓝采和、张果老、何
xiān gū hán xiāng zǐ cáo guó jiù hé lǚ dòng bīn bìng chēng wéi bā xiān
仙姑、韩湘子、曹国舅和吕洞宾并称为“八仙”。
yǒu yì tiān bái yún shén xiān zài péng lái xiān dǎo mǔ dān huā shèng kāi de shí
有一天，白云神仙在蓬莱仙岛牡丹花盛开的时
hou yāo qǐng bā xiān yì qǐ lái shǎng huā bā xiān hěn gāo xìng de dā
候，邀请八仙一起来赏花，八仙很高兴地答
ying le
应了。

zài yàn huì shang tiě guǎi lǐ tí yì qù qí tā dì fang yóu wán lǚ
在宴会上，铁拐李提议去其他地方游玩。吕
dòng bīn shuō rú guǒ jīng guò dà hǎi de huà dà jiā bù néng zuò chuán bì xū píng
洞宾说如果经过大海的话，大家不能坐船，必须凭
jiè zì jǐ de fǎ shù yuè guò dà hǎi dà jiā hěn zàn tóng tā de zhè ge tí yì
借自己的法术越过大海，大家很赞同他的这个提议。

他们一行人来到大海边，每人都展现自己的法术，海面上顿时浪花翻腾，巨大的海浪震动了东海龙王的宫殿。东海龙王派遣侍卫出来查看，知道了是八仙在斗法。东海龙王过来劝阻八仙不要玩闹，还把蓝采和抓走了。其他神仙看到蓝采和被抓走了，于是，大开杀戒。把龙王的儿子都杀掉了。

东海龙王非常愤怒，请来南海、北海、西海龙王，掀起巨大风浪试图淹死这些神仙。忽然，水面上出现了一道金色的光芒，大浪中间出现了一条道路。原来曹国舅手里拿的白云板有避开海水的神力，波涛再怎么汹涌，也拿他们没有办法。四海龙王见此情景，十分恼怒。他们又调动兵将准备再战，这时南海观音出面调和，要求东海龙王释放蓝采和，并让八仙给龙王道

qiàn jīng guò tiáo jiě shuāng fāng zhōng yú tíng zhàn le zuì hòu bā xiān
歉。经过调解，双方终于停战了。最后，八仙

gào bié guān yīn qiāo qiāo de lí kāi le
告别观音，悄悄地离开了。

According to Chinese legend, Tieguai Li, Han Zhongli, Lan Caihe, Zhang Guolao, He Xiangu, Han Xiangzi, Cao Guojiu and Lü Dongbin are called "the Eight Immortals". One day, Baiyun God invited the Eight Immortals to come to Penglai Island (a fabled abode of immortals) where peony bloomed to enjoy the flowers. The eight immortals agreed.

While in the party, Tieguai Li suggested to travel to other places for fun. Then Lü Dongbin said if they needed to travel across the sea, they must go across it by their magic power, not the boat. All of them agreed.

When they came by the sea, each of them showed their own magic power. Instantly, the sea waves were roaring, which shook the East Sea Dragon Palace. Dragon King of the East Sea sent his soldiers to check what happened. It turned out that the Eight Immortals were exercising their magic powers against each other. Dragon King of the East Sea came over to dissuade them but took Lan Caihe away, which annoyed the other gods of the Eight Immortals to fight with him, which resulted in the death of his son.

Dragon King of the East Sea was so furious that he invited his brothers from the South Sea，North Sea and West Sea. They roused huge storms to try to cover those immortals. All of a sudden，a golden light shone beneath the sea. In the middle of the sea there appeared a road. It was Cao Guojiu who used his ritual baton，a magic power tool to create the road. No matter how fierce the waves were，those immortals were not afraid. Seeing this scene，the four Dragon Kings all felt annoyed that they decided to send many more soldiers to fight back. At that time, Goddess Guanyin of the South Sea appeared and persuaded the two parties to stop fighting. On one hand, she required Dragon King of the East Sea to set Lan Caihe free, on the other hand, she advised the Eight Immortals to apologize to the Dragon King. In the end，the Eight Immortals departed with Goddess Guanyin of the South Sea and left secretly.

Story Comment

八仙过海的神话故事，影响很广。后人将其用来形容凭借自己能力去创造奇迹。有“八仙过海、各显神通”、“八仙过海、各凭本事”的说法。

The myth of the Eight Immortals crossing the sea was popular. People use this story to describe a person creating miracles by his own ability. There is a saying “Eight Immortals crossing sea，each shows magic power”.

神女峰

Goddess Peak

chuán shuō zài gǔ shí hou tiān tíng zhōng de yáo chí gōng lǐ zhù zhe xī
传说在古时候，天庭中的瑶池宫里住着西

wáng mǔ de dì èr shí sān gè nǚ ér míng jiào yáo jī yáo jī cí bēi shàn
王母的第二十三个女儿，名叫瑶姬。瑶姬慈悲善

liáng hái xué huì le biàn huà wú qióng de xiān shù bèi fēng wéi yún huá fū
良，还学会了变化无穷的仙术，被封为云华夫

rén zhuān mén fù zé jiào dǎo tóng nán yù nǚ yáo jī cháng nián zài tiān gōng
人，专门负责教导童男玉女。瑶姬长年在天宫

lǐ jū zhù jiù hěn kě wàng néng gòu dào qí tā dì fang kàn kan
里居住，就很渴望能够到其他地方看看。

yì tiān yáo jī dài zhe shí jǐ gè jiě mèi qiāo qiāo de lí kāi xiān gōng
一天，瑶姬带着十几个姐妹悄悄地离开仙宫，

lái dào le dōng hǎi dàn shì tā kàn dào le dà hǎi de kuáng fēng bào yǔ gěi
来到了东海。但是，她看到了大海的狂风暴雨给

rén men zào chéng yán zhòng zāi nàn de shí hou tā xīn lǐ shí fēn shāng xīn
人们造成严重灾难的时候，她心里十分伤心。
tā jué dìng yào jìn quán lì xiāo chú rén jiān de kǔ nàn wèi rén mín zào fú
她决定要尽全力消除人间的苦难，为人民造福。

yáo jī suí jí dài lǐng jiě mèi men chū le dōng hǎi yí lù xiàng xī bian
瑶姬随即带领姐妹们出了东海，一路向西边
fēi qù dāng yáo jī lái dào yún yǔ máng máng de wū shān de shí hou kàn
飞去。当瑶姬来到云雨茫茫的巫山的时候，看
jiàn shí èr tiáo xiōng è de jiāo lóng zhèng zài huò hài bǎi xìng yáo jī fēi
见十二条凶恶的蛟龙正在祸害百姓。瑶姬非
cháng fèn nù tā biàn huà chéng yì tiáo shēn xíng páng dà de yóu lóng jiǎo
常愤怒。她变化成一条身形庞大的游龙，搅
dòng tiān kōng de yún duǒ chà nà jiān tiān léi gǔn gǔn wū yún mì bù dì
动天空的云朵。刹那间，天雷滚滚，乌云密布，地
dòng shān yáo
动山摇。

děng dào fēng píng làng jìng de shí hou shí èr tiáo jiāo lóng de shī tǐ huà
等到风平浪静的时候，十二条蛟龙的尸体化
zuò le shí èr zuò dà shān dǔ sè le wū xiá cháng jiāng de shuǐ liú dùn
作了十二座大山，堵塞了巫峡、长江的水流。顿
shí jiāng shuǐ sì yì yān mò le shān chuān píng yuán bǎi xìng bèi hóng shuǐ
时，江水四溢，淹没了山川平原，百姓被洪水
juǎn zǒu le yáo jī kàn dào zì jǐ rě xià de huò shì shí fēn nèi jiù tā
卷走了。瑶姬看到自己惹下的祸事，十分内疚。她
yuán lái shì xiǎng zào fú rén men de méi yǒu xiǎng dào fǎn ér gěi bǎi xìng dài
原来是想造福人们的，没有想到反而给百姓带
lái le gèng dà de zāi hài zhè shí zhì shuǐ yīng xióng dà yǔ zhèng cóng
来了更大的灾害。这时，治水英雄大禹正从
huáng hé lái dào cháng jiāng biān shang dǎ suàn zhì lǐ zhè xiōng měng de hóng
黄河来到长江边上，打算治理这凶猛的洪

shuǐ yáo jī suí jí xiǎng dào yào bāng zhù dà yǔ lái zhì lǐ shuǐ huàn yáo
水。瑶姬随即想到要帮助大禹来治理水患。瑶
jī gào su dà yǔ zhì shuǐ de fāng fǎ hái xié zhù tā bǎ nán guān jiā yǐ guàn
姬告诉大禹治水的方法，还协助他把难关加以贯
tōng shū dǎo shǐ dé bèi dǔ sè de shuǐ liú néng gòu shùn chàng de tōng guò
通疏导，使得被堵塞的水流能够顺畅地通过。
dà yǔ píng jiè cōng huì yǔ yì lì hé rén men yì qǐ qí xīn xié lì ér qiě
大禹凭借聪慧与毅力，和人们一起齐心协力，而且
dé dào shén xiān yáo jī de bāng zhù tā zhì lǐ hóng shuǐ shí sān nián zhōng yú
得到神仙瑶姬的帮助，他治理洪水十三年，终于
huò dé le chéng gōng
获得了成功。

shuǐ huàn suī rán dé dào le zhì lǐ dàn shì yáo jī què méi yǒu lí kāi
水患虽然得到了治理，但是，瑶姬却没有离开。
yáo jī ài shàng le sān xiá tā tiān tiān zhàn zài gāo yá shang xiàng yuǎn chù tiào
瑶姬爱上了三峡，她天天站在高崖上向远处眺
wàng zhù shì zhe dà xiá gǔ zhōng wǎng lái de chuán zhī suí shí gěi nà xiē
望，注视着大峡谷中往来的船只，随时给那些
yù dào wēi xiǎn de chuán zhī yǐ bāng zhù tā hái tè yì pài le jǐ bǎi zhī
遇到危险的船只以帮助。她还特意派了几百只
shén niǎo zài xiá gǔ de shàng kōng fēi xiáng lái yǐn dǎo chuán zhī píng ān háng
神鸟，在峡谷的上空飞翔，来引导船只平安航
xíng jiù zhè yàng rì fù yí rì nián fù yì nián yáo jī hé jiě mèi men
行。就这样，日复一日，年复一年，瑶姬和姐妹们
wàng jì le fǎn huí tiān gōng yīn wèi cháng jiǔ de zhàn zài gāo yá shang tiào
忘记了返回天宫。因为长久地站在高崖上眺
wàng tā men jiàn jiàn de huà shēn wéi yí zuò zuò shān fēng yǒng yuǎn de níng
望，她们渐渐地化身为一座座山峰，永远地凝
shì zhe yuǎn fāng
视着远方。

jù shuō yáo jī suǒ zhàn lì de shān fēng wèi zhì zuì gāo měi tiān dì yí
据说，瑶姬所站立的山峰位置最高，每天第一

gè yíng lái zhāo xiá yòu zuì hòu yí gè sòng zǒu xuàn lì de wǎn xiá suǒ yǐ
个迎来朝霞，又最后一个送走绚丽的晚霞。所以

shén nǚ fēng yòu yǒu wàng xiá fēng de měi míng
神女峰又有“望霞峰”的美名。

According to Chinese legend, in ancient times, the twenty-third daughter of the Queen Mother of the West named Yaoji lived in the Yaochi Palace in the heaven. Being a kind and powerful fairy with countless changing magic skills, she was honored as Yunhua lady in charge of tutoring young girls and boys. As Yaoji lived in the heavenly palace all year long, she was eager to travel to other places.

One day, she travelled to the East Sea with dozens of sisters. When she saw the storm in the sea brought severe disaster to the people, she felt distressed. She determined to eliminate the suffering on the earth and bring happiness to people.

Then Yaoji led the sisters out of the East Sea and headed for the west. When they arrived at the cloudy the Wu Mountain, they saw twelve fierce dragons doing harm to the people. Furiously, Yaoji changed into a giant dragon and stirred the clouds in the heaven. In a second, the thunder was rolling, the sky was smothered with black clouds, and the earth was shaking.

When all became calm and tranquil, those twelve dragons were dead and their corpuses changed into twelve mountains which blocked the water flow in the Wu Gorge and the Changjiang River. Instantly, the river flooding all over the mountains and plains. People were washed away by the flood. She was guilty of what she had done. She intended to help people out of the disaster but unexpectedly she brought even greater disaster to them. At that time, the hero Yu came by the Changjiang River planning to tame the fierce flood. Then Yaoji told him the flood-taming method, helped him solve the difficulties, and let the blocked water flow again. With his wisdom and diligence as well as Goddess Yaoji's help and people's support, Yu finally tamed the flood after thirteen years' efforts.

The flood was tamed but Yaoji was not willing to leave. She fell in love with the Three Gorges. She stood on the high cliff to overlook the boats flowing in the valley, offering help for those boats in danger. Purposefully, she sent hundreds of holy birds which hovered over the sky to lead the sailing of boats. In this way, day after day, year after year, Yaoji and her sisters forgot to return to the heavenly palace. As they stood on the high cliff for so long, all of them changed into peaks, staring at the distant place forever.

According to Chinese legend, the cliff where Yaoji stood was the highest one. It's the first to wave at the sunrise everyday and the last to give farewell to the glamorous sunset glow. It had a beautiful name "Wangxia Peak (Peak for watching the Glows)".

故事点评 | Story Comment

在我国神话传说中，神女峰是西王母的小女儿瑶姬的化身，她帮助大禹疏通河道，消除水患。随后她毅然决定留在巫山，为来往船只保平安，因而备受后人尊敬。据说，神女峰位于重庆市巫山县的巫峡大江北岸，慕名前来瞻仰她风采的人络绎不绝。

In Chinese myth, the Goddess Peak is the embodiment of Yaoji, the youngest daughter of the Queen Mother of the West, who helped Yu tame the flood. Later she insisted on staying on the Wu Mountain to protect the boats travelling through the river. She is respected and commemorated by the descendents. According to Chinese legend, the Goddess Peak is located on the north bank of the Wu Gorge River in the Wushan County of the city of Chongqing. Countless people come there to admire and worship her.

神笔马良

Ma Liang and His Magic Brush

chuán shuō yǒu gè hái zi míng jiào mǎ liáng fù mǔ qù shì de zǎo tā
传说有个孩子名叫马良，父母去世得早，他
gěi bié rén fàng niú dǎ chái gē cǎo lái wéi chí shēng huó tā cóng xiǎo xǐ
给别人放牛、打柴、割草来维持生活。他从小喜
huān huà huà kě shì tā qióng de lián yì zhī bǐ yě mǎi bu qǐ tā měi
欢画画，可是，他穷得连一支笔也买不起。他每
tiān zhǐ hǎo yòng shù zhī cǎo gēn miáo huà fēi niǎo yóu yú huā cǎo huà gōng
天只好用树枝、草根描画飞鸟、游鱼、花草。画功
zài zhè zhǒng zì xué zhōng màn màn jìn bù huà de huā niǎo chóng yú xǔ xǔ
在这种自学中慢慢进步，画的花鸟虫鱼栩栩
rú shēng
如生。

yǒu yì tiān wǎn shang mǎ liáng shuì zháo le yí wèi bái hú zi lǎo yé
有一天晚上，马良睡着了。一位白胡子老爷

ye sòng gěi tā yì zhī jīn càn càn de huà bǐ tā fēi cháng gāo xìng dào le
爷送给他一支金灿灿的画笔，他非常高兴。到了
dì èr tiān mǎ liáng yòng zhè zhī bǐ huà huà méi xiǎng dào qí jì fā shēng
第二天，马良用这支笔画画，没想到奇迹发生
le tā huà niǎo niǎo huì fēi huà yú yú huì wán shuǐ wú lùn tā huà
了。他画鸟，鸟会飞；画鱼，鱼会玩水。无论他画
shén me dōu néng mǎ shàng biàn chéng zhēn de dōng xi tā kāi xīn jí le
什么都能马上变成真的东西，他开心极了。
cóng cǐ mǎ liáng měi tiān wèi cūn lǐ de qióng rén huà lí bà gēng niú shuǐ
从此，马良每天为村里的穷人画犁耙、耕牛、水
chē shí mò huà guò zhī hòu zhè xiē gōng jù jiù biàn chéng zhēn de néng
车、石磨。画过之后，这些工具就变成真的，能
ná lái gàn huó la
拿来干活啦。

xiāng lín cūn zhuāng zhù zhe yí gè tān lán de dà cái zhǔ tā zhī dào zhè
相邻村庄住着一个贪婪的大财主，他知道这
jiàn shì qing hòu wēi bī mǎ liáng huà jīn shān huà jīn yuán bǎo dàn shì mǎ
件事情后，威逼马良画金山，画金元宝。但是，马
liáng jù jué wèi cái zhǔ zuò huà cái zhǔ jiù bǎ mǎ liáng guān jìn mǎ jiù
良拒绝为财主作画。财主就把马良关进马厩，
xiǎng bǎ tā dòng sǐ è sǐ shéi zhī mǎ liáng yòng shén bǐ huà le shāo
想把他冻死、饿死。谁知马良用神笔画了烧
bǐng huǒ lú mǎ liáng chī de bǎo bǎo de fáng wū lǐ kǎo de nuǎn hōng hōng
饼、火炉，马良吃得饱饱的，房屋里烤得暖烘烘
de tā zài mǎ jiù lǐ shuì zháo le
的。他在马厩里睡着了。

cái zhǔ méi yǒu bàn fǎ wèi le duó qǔ shén bǐ tā jué dìng bǎ mǎ liáng
财主没有办法，为了夺取神笔，他决定把马良
shā diào kě shì dāng cái zhǔ dài zhe hěn duō rén lái zhuō ná mǎ liáng shí
杀掉。可是，当财主带着很多人来捉拿马良时，

què fā xiàn mǎ jiù lǐ kōng wú yì rén zhī kàn dào dōng miàn qiáng bì shang kào
却发现马厩里空无一人，只看到东面墙壁上靠

zhe yí jià tī zi cōng míng de mǎ liáng chèn zhe tiān hēi pá shàng zhè jià
着一架梯子。聪明的马良趁着天黑，爬上这架

tī zi fān guò yuàn qiáng táo zǒu le cái zhǔ jí máng pá shàng tī zi qù
梯子，翻过院墙逃走了。财主急忙爬上梯子去

zhuī gǎn hái méi pá shàng liǎng sān bù jiù shuāi xià lái le yuán lái zhè
追赶，还没爬上两三步，就摔下来了。原来，这

tī zi shì mǎ liáng yòng shén bǐ huà chū lái de
梯子是马良用神笔画出来的。

According to Chinese legend, there was a boy named Ma Liang who lost his parents early and made a living by looking after cows, chopping wood and cutting grass for others. He loved drawing but he was too poor to buy a pen. Every day he used branches or grass roots to draw flying birds, fish, flowers, grasses. By self study, his drawing skills were improved. The flowers, birds, worms and fish he drew were true to life.

One night, after Ma Liang fell asleep, he dreamed an old man with white beard sent him a shining golden pen which delighted him. The next day, he used this pen to draw birds and the birds could fly. He drew fish and the fish could swim. Whatever he drew could become real. He was joyful. Since then, Ma Liang drew the plow and harrow, farm cattle, waterwheel and stone mill every day every day for the poor in the village. All became real and could be used for labor work.

A greedy rich man in the nearby village who knew the whole thing threatened Ma Liang to draw gold mountains and gold ingots. But Ma Liang refused. Then the man locked Ma Liang into a stable to starve and freeze him to death. Ma Liang used the magic brush to draw baked rolls and a stove. He enjoyed the food and slept sweetly in the warm stable.

The rich man had no other way but to kill him. When the rich man led many people to catch Ma Liang, they only saw a ladder leaning against the east side of the wall in the yard. In the dark, Ma Liang had already climbed over the wall with the ladder. The rich man hurried to climb on the ladder to chase him. In less than two or three steps, he fell down. The ladder on which the rich man stood was drawn by Ma Liang with the magic brush.

生难字/词注解 | Notes

栩栩如生：形容生动传神的样子。

True to life: Like real.

马厩：马棚，泛指牲口棚。

Stable: A building in which horses are kept.

Story Comment

马良凭借勤奋、智慧与努力自学成才，用神笔造福百姓，勇敢反抗恶霸，展现了他的高尚人格和无私无畏的精神。

With his diligence, wisdom and hard work, Ma Liang became a talent by self-study. He used the magic brush to help people and was brave enough to fight against the evil, which reflected his noble character and selfless spirit.

田螺姑娘

The River Snail Maiden

hěn jiǔ yǐ qián hóu guān xiàn yǒu gè míng jiào xiè duān de nián qīng rén
很久以前，侯官县有个名叫谢端的年轻人。
zài tā hěn xiǎo de shí hou fù mǔ jiù sǐ le zhǐ liú xià tā yí gè rén shēng
在他很小的时候父母就死了，只留下他一个人生
huó yóu yú shēng huó pín kùn tā yì zhí méi yǒu jié hūn kě shì tā méi
活。由于生活贫困，他一直没有结婚。可是他没
yǒu yīn cǐ xiāo chén fán mèn réng rán měi tiān qín kěn láo zuò
有因此消沉烦闷，仍然每天勤恳劳作。

yì tiān tā zài tián lǐ jiǎn dào yì zhī tè bié dà de tián luó jiù bǎ
一天，他在田里捡到一只特别大的田螺，就把
tā dài huí jiā yǎng zài shuǐ gāng lǐ zhī hòu jiù fā shēng lìng tā jīng qí de
它带回家养在水缸里。之后就发生令他惊奇的
shì qing tā bái tiān qù dì lǐ láo dòng huí jiā hòu jiù huì kàn dào zào tái
事情。他白天去地里劳动，回家后就会看到灶台

shang fàng zhe yǐ zuò hǎo le de xiāng pēn pēn de fàn cài gāng kāi shǐ de shí
上放着已做好了的香喷喷的饭菜。刚开始的时
hou tā hái yǐ wéi shì lín jū bāng tā zuò de jiù dào lín jū jiā qù dào
候，他还以为是邻居帮他做的，就到邻居家去道
xiè kě shì lín jū dōu shuō bú shì tā men zuò de xiè duān hěn nà mèn
谢。可是，邻居都说不是他们做的。谢端很纳闷，
tā hào qí dào dǐ shì shéi wèi tā zuò de fàn cài yú shì tā xiǎng le yí
他好奇到底是谁为他做的饭菜。于是，他想了一
gè zhǔ yi
个主意。

dì èr tiān xiè duān xiàng wǎng cháng yí yàng káng zhe chú tou xià dì
第二天，谢端像往常一样，扛着锄头下地
qù láo dòng rán hòu yòu fǎn huí jiā duǒ zài mén wài tōu tōu de kàn shì shéi zài
去劳动，然后又返回家，躲在门外偷偷地看是谁在
wū lǐ gàn huó bù yí huìr tā kàn dào yí gè nián qīng měi lì de gū
屋里干活。不一会儿，他看到一个年轻美丽的姑
niang cóng shuǐ gāng lǐ huǎn huǎn zǒu chū lái zhè gū niang lái dào zào qián
娘从水缸里缓缓走出来。这姑娘来到灶前，
hěn shú liàn de shāo huǒ zuò cài zhǔ fàn hěn kuài jiù shāo hǎo le yì zhuō zi de
很熟练地烧火做菜煮饭，很快就烧好了一桌子的
fàn cài fàn cài zuò hǎo zhī hòu gū niang zhèng yào zǒu jìn shuǐ gāng lǐ qù
饭菜。饭菜做好之后，姑娘正要走进水缸里去
shí xiè duān fēi kuài de pǎo jìn wū lǐ lā zhù gū niáng de yī fu zhuī wèn
时，谢端飞快地跑进屋里，拉住姑娘的衣服追问
tā de lái lì gū niang méi yǒu bàn fǎ zhi hǎo bǎ shí qíng gào su tā
她的来历，姑娘没有办法，只好把实情告诉他。

yuán lái zhè wèi gū niang shì tiān shàng de xiān nǚ tiān dì zhī dào
原来，这位姑娘是天上的仙女。天帝知道
xiè duān de zāo yù hěn tóng qíng tā suǒ yǐ tā pài xiān nǚ xià fán bāng
谢端的遭遇，很同情他。所以，他派仙女下凡帮

zhù xiè duān chéng jiā lì yè xiàn zài tiān jī xiè lòu xiān nǚ bì xū huí dào
助谢端成家立业。现在天机泄露，仙女必须回到
tiān tíng lín zǒu de shí hou xiān nǚ bǎ tián luó ké zèng sòng gěi le xiè
天庭。临走的时候，仙女把田螺壳赠送给了谢
duān hái shuō zhè lǐ miàn yǒu chī bù wán de liáng shi rán hòu piāo rán
端，还说这里面有吃不完的粮食，然后飘然
lí qù
离去。

cóng cǐ xiè duān bǐ yǐ qián gèng jiā chī kǔ nài láo xīn qín gēng
从此，谢端比以前更加吃苦耐劳，辛勤耕
zhòng méi guò jǐ nián xiè duān biàn chéng jiā lì yè le yì jiā rén guò
种。没过几年，谢端便成家立业了，一家人过
shàng le xìng fú měi mǎn de shēng huó
上了幸福美满的生活。

Long time ago, in Houguan County, there was a young man named Xie Duan whose parents died when he was a little boy. Because of the poor life, he could not get married. But he was not gloomy. Every day he worked hard.

One day, he picked up a large river snail. He brought it back home and kept it in the water vat. Then something surprising happened. During the daytime, the young man went to the field to work but when he returned home at night, he found there were so many delicious foods on the kitchen stove. At first, the young man thought it was made by his neighbor, so he came to the neighbor's to thank them. But the neighbors denied. The young man was puzzled and really wanted to know who did it. Then he had an idea.

The next day, he went to the field with his hoe as usual but returned secretly and hid behind the door to see who would do the cooking. After a while, he saw a beautiful young lady came out of the water vat and went to the kitchen stove for cooking. In no time, the table was full of food. After the food was prepared already, the lady was about to go back to the water vat when Xie Duan ran into the house quickly and stopped the young lady to ask where she came from. The young lady had no other choice but to tell him the truth.

It turned out that the Emperor of Heaven felt sympathy for the young man and sent the fairy to help him get married and have a career. Now the truth was known. The fairy must return to the Heaven. Before she left, the fairy gave the young man a shell of river snail, saying there was endless food in it.

Since then, Xie Duan became more diligent, industrious and hardworking. A few years later, he got married and led a happy family life.

生难字/词注解 | Note

田螺：软体动物，壳圆锥形，触角长，生长在淡水中。

River snail: A small soft creature with a hard round shell on its back that moves very slowly and often eats garden plants.

故事点评 | Story Comment

谢端从小父母双亡，孤苦伶仃但仍然安分守己、勤奋工作。天帝同情他的遭遇，就派仙女下凡给予他帮助。这个优美动人的神话故事告诉我们上天会眷顾德行高尚的人，勤劳、善良的人总会得到意想不到的福慧和恩泽。

Although Xie Duan's parents died when he was a little boy, he still behaved himself and worked hard every day. The Emperor of Heaven felt sympathy for him and sent a fairy to help him. This touching myth tells us god would help those noble men. Those diligent and kind people would get unexpected luck and good wishes.

百鸟朝凤

Hundred Birds Paying Homage to the Phoenix

zài gǔ shí hou　jù shuō fèng huáng kāi shǐ shí zhǐ shì yì zhǒng pǔ tōng
在古时候，据说凤凰开始时只是一种普通
de xiǎo niǎo　hé qí tā de niǎo bìng méi yǒu shén me chā bié　tā de yǔ máo
的小鸟，和其他的鸟并没有什么差别。它的羽毛
yě hěn píng cháng　méi yǒu xiàng xiàn zài zhè yàng de xuàn lì duó mù　guāng cǎi
也很平常，没有像现在这样的绚丽夺目、光彩
zhào rén　kě shì　fèng huáng yǒu yí gè yōu diǎn　jiù shì hěn qín láo　tā
照人。可是，凤凰有一个优点，就是很勤劳。它
bú xiàng bié de niǎo nà yàng chī bǎo le jiù dào chù fēi lái fēi qù de wán shuǎ
不像别的鸟那样吃饱了就到处飞来飞去地玩耍，
ér shì cóng zǎo dào wǎn zhěng tiān de cāo láo máng lù　tā píng shí jiāng kě
而是从早到晚整天地操劳忙碌。它平时将可

yǐ chī de guǒ zi mǐ lì děng shí wù dōu jiǎn qǐ lái hěn xiǎo xīn de zhù
以吃的果子、米粒等食物都捡起来，很小心地贮
cáng zài shù dòng lǐ zhè yàng měi tiān yì diǎn diǎn de jī lěi liáng shi shù
藏在树洞里。这样每天一点点地积累，粮食数
liàng yě màn màn de zēng duō le
量也慢慢地增多了。

qí tā xiǎo niǎo kàn dào fèng huáng zhè yàng yòng xīn de jī zǎn shí wù
其他小鸟看到凤凰这样用心地积攒食物，
hěn bù yǐ wéi rán tā men jué de tiān dì zhī jiān zhè me dà shù lín zhè me
很不以为然。它们觉得天地之间这么大，树林这么
duō suí shí suí dì dōu kě yǐ xún zhǎo dào kě yǐ chōng jī de shí wù hé
多，随时随地都可以寻找到可以充饥的食物，何
kǔ yào zhè yàng tiān tiān qù jī zǎn qǐ lái ne zhè bú shì dà shǎ guā ma
苦要这样天天去积攒起来呢。这不是大傻瓜吗？
fèng huáng bìng bú zài hu xiǎo niǎo men de kàn fǎ ér shì zài bié rén de cháo
凤凰并不在乎小鸟们的看法，而是在别人的嘲
xiào zhōng jì xù zhe tā men de xīn qín láo zuò
笑中继续着它们的辛勤劳作。

yǒu yì nián sēn lín lǐ fā shēng dà hàn cǎo mù shù yè dōu gān kū
有一年，森林里发生大旱，草木树叶都干枯
le shù shang zài yě méi yǒu jié guǒ zi xiǎo niǎo men zhǎo bú dào shí wù
了，树上再也没有结果子，小鸟们找不到食物。
dà jiā è de tóu hūn yǎn huā kuài zhī chēng bú xià qù le zhè shí fèng
大家饿得头昏眼花，快支撑不下去了。这时，凤
huáng jí máng dài lǐng dà jiā fēi dào nà ge cáng yǒu liáng shi de shù dòng bǎ
凰急忙带领大家飞到那个藏有粮食的树洞，把
zì jǐ duō nián jī cún xià lái de gān guǒ hé cǎo zǐ ná chū lái fēn gěi dà jiā
自己多年积存下来的干果和草籽拿出来分给大家。
niǎo ér men kàn dào shù dòng lǐ yǒu zhè me duō de liáng shi dōu hěn gāo xìng
鸟儿们看到树洞里有这么多的粮食，都很高兴，

dà jiā yì qǐ fēn xiǎng shí wù jiù zhè yàng gòng dù le nán guān
大家一起分享食物，就这样共渡了难关。

hàn zāi guò hòu wèi le gǎn xiè fèng huáng de jiù mìng zhī ēn niǎo ér
旱灾过后，为了感谢凤凰的救命之恩，鸟儿
men dōu cóng zì jǐ shēn shang xuǎn le yì gēn zuì piào liang de yǔ máo bá xià
们都从自己身上选了一根最漂亮的羽毛拔下
lái zhì chéng le yí jiàn guāng cǎi yào yǎn de bǎi niǎo yī jìng xiàn gěi le
来，制成了一件光彩耀眼的百鸟衣敬献给了
fèng huáng bìng yí zhì tuī jǔ tā wéi bǎi niǎo zhī wáng cóng cǐ yǐ hòu
凤凰，并一致推举它为百鸟之王。从此以后，
fèng huáng bù jǐn yōng yǒu le shì jiè shang zuì piào liang xuàn lì de yǔ
凤凰不仅拥有了世界上最漂亮、炫丽的羽
máo ér qiě měi féng fèng huáng shēng rì de shí hou sì miàn bā fāng de
毛，而且每逢凤凰生日的时候，四面八方的
niǎo ér dōu huì fēi lái xiàng fèng huáng biǎo shì zhù hè tā men wéi zài fèng
鸟儿都会飞来向凤凰表示祝贺。它们围在凤
huáng de zhōu wéi gāo xìng de chàng zhe gē tiào zhe wǔ xiàn gěi fèng huáng
凰的周围，高兴地唱着歌，跳着舞，献给凤凰
zuì zhēn chéng de zhù yuàn zhè jiù xíng chéng le hòu lái de bǎi niǎo cháo fèng
最真诚的祝愿。这就形成了后来的百鸟朝凤
de chuán shuō
的传说。

In ancient times, according to Chinese legend, phoenix was a kind of ordinary small bird. Its feathers were very common without a glamorous look. But it was diligent, unlike other birds flying around for fun once the stomach was full. It kept working from day to night, picking up nuts, grains, etc., and storing them in a cave. The food was accumulated gradually in this way day after day.

Other birds looked down upon what the phoenix did. Because they believed the world was big enough with so many woods to find food. Why should they take efforts to collect food every day? It seemed stupid. The phoenix did not care what other birds thought. In their tease, the phoenix went on working hard.

One year, a severe drought happened in the forest. All the grass and woods withered. There was no fruit left on the trees. Birds flew around for food but could find nothing. As the birds were nearly starved to death, the phoenix hurried there and led the birds to the cave where the food was stored. The phoenix shared the dry fruits and grass seeds with all the birds, helping them go through the disaster. All of them felt happy and contented.

After the drought, to thank the phoenix, all the birds plucked their most beautiful feather and made a shining and glamorous clothes for it. They all selected it as the king of the birds. Since then, not only did the phoenix have the most beautiful feathers in the world, but all the birds flew together to celebrate the phoenix's birthday. They flew around the phoenix, singing and dancing, making the best wishes for it, which formed the legend story of hundred birds paying homage to the phoenix.

故事点评 | Story Comment

百鸟朝凤，也称作百鸟朝王，这一神话故事在千年的流传中具有丰富文化内涵。在古代传说中，凤凰就是神鸟，是美好吉祥的象征。后来，在人们心中，凤凰不再仅仅是一只神鸟了，它是“百鸟之王”，成了尊贵与权力的象征，用来比喻君主圣明，天下归顺，以及用来表达人们对和平、幸福生活的向往。

Hundred birds paying homage to the phoenix is also called “hundred birds paying homage to the king”. In the ancient legend, the phoenix was a holy bird which symbolized luck and happiness. Later, in people's heart, the phoenix was not just a holy bird but the king of hundred birds which stood for dignity and power. People use hundred birds paying homage to the phoenix to imply a wise emperor under whose leadership, people live a harmonious life. It could also show people's wish for a peaceful and happy life.

后 记

中国神话故事源远流长，丰富多彩。作为中华民族童年时代的产物，它们以浪漫史诗的形式再现了远古时期人们最初的社会生活和精神面貌。这些神话传说所展露出的奇异瑰丽的世界，让我们体会到人类对大自然的好奇、对英雄的敬仰、对苦难的斗争、对美好生活的向往，以及对恶势力的憎恶等丰富细腻的感情。直到今天，那些神话传说丰盈神奇的艺术境界和奋发图强的进取精神，仍然深深地感染和激励着我们。

中国神话故事不仅是中华文明产生和发展的源头，也是中华民族文化精神与核心价值的生动体现。它在关怀生命、教益人生与构建社会伦理秩序等方面都具有巨大的普适性价值，具有永恒的艺术魅力。

作为一名教授和研究中国文学和文化的教师，我深切地感受到承担文化传承与创新的历史责任和使命。因此，聚焦中国传统文化，挖掘传统文化中最有价值、最具普适性精神内涵的精品，是我思考和从事华文教育教学工作和研究的一个重要维度。因为重现和阅读它们，我们得到的不仅是美学上的享受，更能对中华文化、中国形象产生更为深刻的认识。

在书稿即将付梓之时，在此，我向一直关心和支持我的领导、师长、亲友深表感谢。衷心感谢学校、学院各级领导、同事们的关心与支持，他们为我提供较好的科研平台，使我能够安心工作与著述，使本书能够顺利出版。衷心感谢浙江大学出版社的包灵灵女士、宋旭华先生等人，对本书做了精心指点，提出了宝贵的建议；衷心感谢泰国宋卡王子大学的林桃源、陈美琳、温玛丽、蔡青青、萧丽华、明明等 34 名同学，她们对我设计的关于文学经典鉴赏、汉语学习认知的调研工作不辞繁难地积极参与、乐在其中；感谢刘金程先生等人谋划、绘制了本书插图；我校汉语国际教育专业的学生施育恒、石政、刘林搜集、整理了相关资料，陈玉、崔艳萍对文稿做了校对工作，在此一并感谢。

我还要衷心感谢我的父母、哥嫂、其他亲人，他们宅心仁厚、安分守己和勤勉耐苦的美德，深深地影响并成就了我。同时，我还要感谢我的爱人和我刚满两周岁的小宝贝。有爱才有家，有家才有梦，有梦才能走更远。感谢所有亲友的一路陪伴，他们的不离不弃，使我克服一个个难题，坚持不懈地努力与前行。

本书选取的这些神话故事，基本上是流传久远，普通老百姓耳熟能详的经典故事。我们希望这些故事能重述给不同国界、不同文化、各个年龄段的读者。由于时间仓促，难免会有疏漏和错误之处，敬请各位专家、学者不吝批评指正。希望在未来听取各方面的意见后，能有机会对本书加以修订。

李火秀

2016年2月8日于赣州

Postscript

With a long history, as the products of Chinese nation's childhood, the rich Chinese myths show the social and spiritual life of primitive people in the form of romantic epic. These myths give us a glorious and glamorous world in which we can feel people's curiosity towards nature, worship towards heroes, fighting against troubles, wishes for a good life and hatreds towards the vicious power. Till now, the rich and magical artistic beauty and enterprising spirits in these myths still inspire and motivate us.

Chinese myths are not only the origin of Chinese civilization, but also the representatives of Chinese nation's cultural spirit and core values. They care about life, instruct people how to live and construct an orderly society. With everlasting artistic charm, Chinese myths are always full of universal values.

As a teacher doing studies on Chinese literature and culture, I deeply feel the duty and responsibility of passing on cultural evolution and creation. So, focusing on Chinese traditional culture, picking out the most valuable, suitable works is one of my jobs. Reading them and enjoying them will not only give you pleasure but also impress you with Chinese culture and Chinese image.

Now the book is going to be published, and I want to extend

sincere gratitude to my dear leaders, teachers and friends who have been supporting me all the time. I would like to thank leaders and colleagues in my university and college for their help and care in providing me with such a good research platform which enables me to focus on my book and get it published. Heartfelt thanks also go to Ms. Bao Lingling and Mr. Song Xuhua from Zhejiang University Press for their meticulous guidance and valuable suggestions. I'm grateful to the 34 students from Prince of Songkla University in Thailand: Lin Taoyuan, Chen Meilin, Wen Mali, Cai Qingqing, Xiao Lihua, Ming Ming and so on, for their cooperation in my survey on literature classic appreciation and Chinese learning cognition. Thanks go to Liu Jincheng for drawing illustrations for this book and Shi Yuheng, Shi Zheng, Liu Lin, students of our program of Teaching Chinese to Speakers of Other Languages, for doing me great favors in collecting and sorting documents. Gratitude goes to Chen Yu and Cui Yangping, students of our program, for their proofreading of this book.

I also want to thank my parents, brother and sister-in-law, and other relatives because their kindness and diligence have influenced and made me who I am. I also want to show my gratitude to my husband and my two-year-old baby daughter. Where there is love, there is home. A lovely home stimulates one to dream and achieve it. Thanks go to all the relatives and friends for their companion which helps me overcome challenges one by one and keep moving forward.

Chinese myths selected in this book are the best-known classic stories which are familiar to common Chinese people. We hope these stories can be told to readers from different nations, with different cultures and in different ages. Due to the time rush, there may be many careless omissions and errors, and we sincerely expect that experts and scholars would leave their advice. We hope that in the future there is chance for us to revise this book after receiving comments and advice.

Li Huoxiu

February 8th, 2016, Ganzhou

图书在版编目(CIP)数据

中国经典神话故事：英汉对照/ 李火秀，邓琳编著.
—杭州：浙江大学出版社，2016.9(2017.11 重印)

ISBN 978-7-308-16071-1

Ⅰ.①中… Ⅱ.①李…②邓… Ⅲ.①英语—汉语—对照读物②神话—作品集—中国 Ⅳ.①H319.4：I

中国版本图书馆 CIP 数据核字（2016）第 173398 号

中国经典神话故事：英汉对照

李火秀 邓 琳 编著

责任编辑 包灵灵
责任校对 董 唯
封面设计 杭州林智广告有限公司
出版发行 浙江大学出版社
（杭州市天目山路 148 号 邮政编码 310007）
（网址：http://www.zjupress.com）
排　　版 杭州林智广告有限公司
印　　刷 杭州日报报业集团盛元印务有限公司
开　　本 889mm×1194mm 1/32
印　　张 6.75
字　　数 197 千
版 印 次 2016 年 9 月第 1 版 2017 年 11 月第 2 次印刷
书　　号 ISBN 978-7-308-16071-1
定　　价 35.00 元
